THE WONDERS OF FUNGI

Everywhere you go, you are surrounded by fungi: the mushrooms beneath a rotten log, the decay of the log itself, the yeast that makes your bread rise, the mold that spoils it, the similar mold that makes the penicillin your doctor often prescribes for illness.

Fungi have lived for millions of years, under every condition and climate, and they may be the only living things that will be found on Mars. Their spores can travel thousands of miles and start life anew. They form a vital part of our world. Yet we seldom think about them, just as we seldom think about the important algae.

And just as Lucy Kavaler brought algae to the consciousness of thousands of readers through her book, *The Wonders of Algae*, so she does for fungi in this new volume.

THE WONDERS OF FUNGI

LUCY KAVALER

Illustrated with photographs
and with drawings by
RICHARD OTT

THE JOHN DAY COMPANY
NEW YORK
an Intext publisher

Ninth Impression

The John Day Company, 257 Park Avenue South, New York N.Y. 10010

ISBN: 0-381-99770-7   Reinforced Edition

Published on the same day in Canada by Longman   Canada Limited.

Library of Congress Catalogue Card Number: 64-10450

Manufactured in the United States of America

For my nieces
Janet, Nancy and Katherine

CONTENTS

1·

THE PLANT THAT IS NOT GREEN

WHAT WILL the spacemen see when they step out onto the hard, dry surface of Mars? They will not find strange human creatures, or animals or even stately trees. It is quite possible, however, that they will bend down and scrape tiny plants off the barren rock.

These may be very much like the simple, primitive plants we have on earth. Some of them will probably belong to a group of living things called fungi. This word is pronounced FUN-jy, (second syllable rhymes with "sky") and it is the plural of fungus, which is spoken the way it is spelled.

Everywhere you go, you are surrounded by fungi. You take a walk through the woods. The mushrooms growing beneath the rotten log are fungi. And the log itself is rotten as a result of the work of other fungi. You go into your kitchen to get a slice of bread. Yeast, which is also a fungus, made the dough rise. If you do not eat the bread quickly enough, a fungus will do so instead. The mold which forms on the loaf is actually eating it. When you are sick, the doctor comes and gives you a shot of penicillin. This drug, too, is made from a fungus.

The story of fungi takes us back in time from the age of space travel and wonder drugs to prehistoric days. Remains of these plants have been found in dinosaur pits. And fungi were not new even then. Bits of them can still be seen stuck inside shells and sponges that are hundreds of millions of years old. A scientist discovered one in a piece of petrified wood that had been preserved through the centuries. Ferns in the ancient jungles of 200 million years ago were damaged by a fungus disease that exists today.

Gradually fungi spread over the face of the globe. No climate has been too bad for them. Some molds grow at blistering temperatures of 130° Fahrenheit. Cold only seems to kill fungi; it does not really finish them off. They stop growing, but they do not die. Like the princess in the old fairy tale, they remain asleep as the years go by . . . until the moment comes for them to awaken. This moment, to be sure, is not brought about by the kiss of the prince, but by the return of just a little warmth. And so fungi can be found in the Arctic wastes, in the jungles of New Guinea, in the sands of the Sahara desert, in the deep caves of Yucatán, in the oceans' depths, in your own backyard.

When you pick up a handful of soil, you are holding thousands of tiny fungi in your fingers. Some of them make the soil fertile so that crops can grow, while others kill those same crops. Some fungi are eaten, and others spoil food. Some make you sick, and others give vitamins and medicines. Some are used to make fabrics out of fibers, and

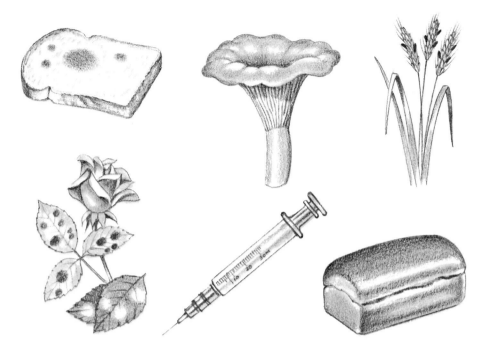

others ruin those very fabrics. No one and nothing is immune.

During the American Revolution fungi rotted the battleships of the proud British Navy. Sixty-six ships had to be scuttled. You might say that these little plants were soldiers in the American Army. In the Civil War the Rebels had trouble with fungi as well as with Union soldiers. Trains left the Deep South carrying supplies for General Robert E. Lee. They never arrived, because the fungi destroyed the wooden ties of the railroad tracks.

On the other hand, fungi have often saved people from starvation. Men lost in the forests have come back telling that they owe their lives to these plants. Nomads traveling through the trackless deserts have eaten them, too. A famous composer recalls that when he was poor and could find no one to listen to his music, he lived on mushrooms gathered in the woods.

The reason for the sharp contrast between good and bad fungi is that there are so many kinds. Most of them are tiny; millions could fit on the head of a pin. Others are tremendous, like the giant mushroom discovered in Minnesota recently. It stood over two feet high and weighed 45 pounds. More than 100,000 different species or types of fungi have been discovered so far. The search is not over. Every year new species are found, as people explore caves, mountains, deserts and jungles. You may soon be hearing about some unusual ones brought back to earth from other planets.

"Before we're through, I think we'll have come upon 250,000 different species," says a mycologist. This is the name given to scientists who work with fungi.

All of these fungi are very different from trees and flowers. They are not a bit like animals either. A number of scientists, therefore, believe that fungi do not belong either to the plant or the animal kingdom. Instead, they are members of a *third* kingdom all by themselves. Other mycologists disagree. You will usually hear fungi described as plants of a strange and unusual type.

As one scientist explained it to his small son: "A fungus is a plant that is not green."

The green color of the higher plants comes from an extremely important substance called chlorophyll. This does much more than just make leaves look pretty. Only plants which have chlorophyll can take in water and carbon dioxide and simple minerals and use them to make their own food. The process by which they do this is known as photosynthesis.

Fungi do not have chlorophyll and cannot make their own food. But this does not mean that they cannot grow. Nature has provided them with ways of surviving. They snatch their food from other plants and from animals. Some fungi fasten onto living plants or animals and obtain nourishment from them. These are called parasites. Others find food in dead bodies or the waste products of living organisms. These are known as saprophytes. Still others can be parasites when living things are around, and saprophytes when they are not. Eating the dead sounds most unpleasant, but none of us would be here today if it were not for the saprophytes.

Can you imagine what the earth would be like if every tree that had ever been knocked down in a storm lay where it had fallen? What would have happened if the remains of dinosaurs, saber-toothed tigers, mammoths and Neanderthal man stayed unchanged? There would be no room on this globe for new trees to grow, or new animals to be born. Every inch of space would be filled forever by the first living things that got here.

What is more, if a few new plants did manage to squeeze in, there would be nothing for them to eat. A flower cannot eat another flower or a blade of grass. It makes its food out of carbon dioxide and simple minerals. A single sunflower needs 14 ounces of carbon dioxide a month. A scientist has figured out that 88,105,726,872 tons of carbon dioxide are taken in each year by the plants that exist on the earth. Only a quarter of this amount can be provided by the atmosphere. The rest comes from decaying plants and animals.

Very early in the history of the earth, fungi and bacteria which could live on dead things appeared. These organisms have a special way of eating. They digest their food in advance. When one of them fastens into a bit of dead wood or a leaf or hair, it quickly releases chemical compounds called enzymes. These are something like the enzymes we have in our digestive systems. The chemicals attack the wood or leaf and break it down until it turns back into the carbon, nitrogen, sulphur and other minerals it was made of in the first place. The fungi eat as much as they can, but there is too much. The leftover minerals go back into the soil and the remaining carbon goes into the air as carbon dioxide. Higher plants use these for food and grow . . . animals eat the plants and grow . . . other animals and human beings eat the animals and the plants and grow. In time, they are eaten by the fungi and bacteria. Those simple organisms die, too, when conditions are unfavorable and in turn are eaten by other members of their own families. Along with all dead things, they are returned to the soil. In this way, the cycle of life on earth goes on and on.

Although the fungi are so important to every living thing, they are extremely simple. A fungus does not have a stem or roots or leaves. It simply has a body and a very strange one at that. This body is made up of tiny threads called hyphae (pronounced HY-fee). These hyphae grow into a tangled mass known as mycelium (my-SEE-li-um). And they grow faster than you would believe possible. Within a single day and night, a colony of fungi can produce more than half a mile of the tiny threadlike cells. That is why molds take over a loaf of bread so quickly.

In order to reproduce, fungi form spores. These are something like the seeds produced by higher plants. But you will never find a flower or tree that can produce as

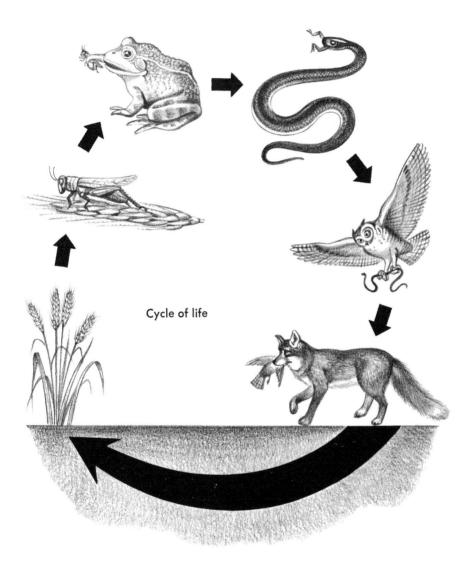

Cycle of life

Fungi and bacteria return all these to earth.

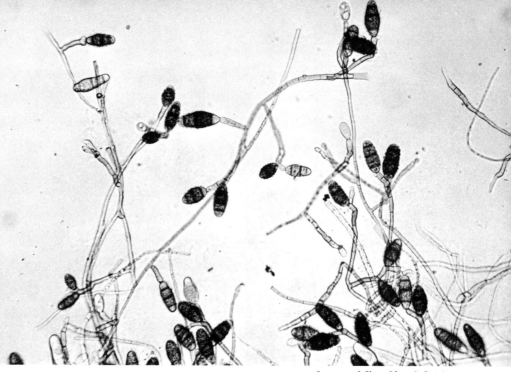

Hyphae and spores as they look under a microscope.

many seeds. A single fungus releases hundreds of *millions* of spores within three or four days. It is lucky for us that most of these spores do not survive. If they did, these tiny plants would take over the world.

As it is, fungi can be found on thousands of different things. They live in logs, bark, cotton fabrics, wool, leather, seeds, manufactured foods, cardboard boxes, cold cream, hair, glue, meat, fruits, milk, drugs, rope and almost anything else you can name. Some species are extremely fussy, however. One of them can grow only on the left hind leg of a particular kind of water beetle. Another lives on the bottom of the leaf of a single type of weed.

16

Although they are primitive plants, fungi like modern products, too. They enjoy jet fuels nearly as much as they do a piece of old wood. Plastics provide them with nourishment, too, and they eat the chemical which makes shower curtains or raincoats soft. Most people think roads crack because of weather and the weight of heavy cars or trucks. That is true, but it is not the whole truth. Again, the fungi are taking the asphalt apart. When you see paint peeling off a house, do not be too quick to blame the rain, wind or snow. The tiny organisms may be the cause.

"Fungi were a hidden menace in the South Pacific," recalls a veteran of World War II. "We would try to radio to other units and the radio wouldn't work. We'd open it up, and sure enough, we'd find fungi inside. They grew on gunsights, binoculars and electrical equipment, and on top of the instrument cases. Our shoes got moldy and so did our clothes. I remember one instruction booklet sent to us from the United States. When we opened it, the paper simply fell apart in our hands. I sometimes wonder what we were supposed to learn from it."

2.

A HUNDRED THOUSAND VARIETIES

FOR MANY CENTURIES people knew what fungi could do without knowing what they were. In 3000 B.C. the pharaohs of Egypt ate bread. Four thousand years ago pictures showing the story of the flood were carved on stone tablets in Assyria. Beer, which is made by the action of yeast, was being taken into the ark. The ancient Greeks suffered from hunger when fungi ruined their crops.

As recently as the early 1800's, Thomas Jefferson was advising his friends in Virginia not to build houses of wood. The boards rotted too quickly in the warm climate, he told them. Even Jefferson did not know that fungi were to blame.

Our understanding of these tiny plants came in the second half of the nineteenth century. At that time a German botanist, Heinrich Anton de Bary, studied and described the many kinds of fungi. He proved that some of them were the "germs" responsible for a number of diseases. In his work he watched fungi grow from spore to mycelium.

The scientists who followed him have divided the 100,000 known species into groups and have given them names. This makes it possible for a mycologist in India and another in Brazil to compare notes. If one of them finds a strange fungus, he can find out quickly if it is really new. The U. S. Government and many universities keep collections of fungi, and have records and descriptions of every fungus that has ever been seen.

Fungi belong to the branch of the plant kingdom called the *Thallophyta*, pronounced tha-LOF-i-ta. Whenever you see this term, you will know that plants without stems, roots or leaves are being described. The Thallophyta are in turn split up into major divisions. The correct word for each division is "phylum" (FY-lum), and fungi belong to the phylum *Eumycophyta* (U-my-co-fi-ta). This phylum is again divided into four classes. Sometimes it is hard to figure out how scientists decided where each fungus was to go.

"Fungi produce different kinds of spores, and in different ways," explains a mycologist. "Some have their spores in a kind of sac, others on special stalks that are shaped like clubs. Each class is made up of those plants that reproduce in roughly the same way. They are often very different in every other particular. The same class can have big members and tiny little ones."

Here are the four main classes of fungi:

One. The *Phycomycetes* (fy-coh-my-SEE-teez)

You can find these fungi practically anywhere — on land and in the sea. Many plant diseases are caused by the

19

phycomycetes. Sometimes they make people sick, too. Certain members of the family fasten onto fish. If you have had a goldfish which died unexpectedly, one of these fungi may have been the cause. Others in the group spoil our food. The common black bread mold is one of these.

But the phycomycetes are not all bad. In fact, we could not do without them. They help to keep the soil fertile. We use them to produce alcohols, acids, and other chemicals. They are important in the making of candy, textiles, paper and medicines.

Two. The *Ascomycetes* (as-koh-my-SEE-teez)

All of mankind is grateful to this group, which contains more than 30,000 species. Its star member produces penicillin. Two very close relatives of that mold give the strong flavor to Roquefort and Camembert cheeses.

Bread, wine and beer are made by the action of yeasts, which are also valuable ascomycetes. Many acids used in soft drinks, foods and industrial products also come from members of this class. If you go to a fine French restaurant, you will see pâté de foie gras on the menu. This dish contains goose liver together with an ascomycete called a truffle. You can be sure that very few of the people who order it realize that they are eating a fungus.

But just as the phycomycetes are not all bad, the ascomycetes are not all good. Some members of this class are responsible for a number of serious illnesses for which no cure is known. The diseases sometimes end in death. These fungi are also to blame for many terrible plant sicknesses, including the one which killed most American chestnut trees. They form the powdery mildew you have surely seen on the roses in the garden. Other ascomycetes make food rotten or moldy, and attack leather, fabric, paper and wood.

Bread mold
(Phycomycete)

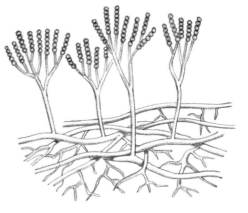

Penicillin mold
(Ascomycete)

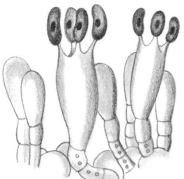

Mushroom reproductive cells
(Basidiomycete)

Slime mold
(Myxomycophyta)

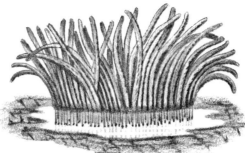

Different types of fungi, greatly enlarged.

Three. The *Basidiomycetes* (ba-sid-ioh-my-SEE-teez)

Next time you are served mushrooms, you can surprise your family by informing them that they are eating basidiomycetes. It would probably be a good thing if basidiomycetes consisted of mushrooms and nothing else. Unfortunately, this class also contains fungi which cause the worst crop diseases. Every year acres and acres of wheat, rye, oats and corn are ruined by infections called rusts and smuts. The lofty oaks and elms in our forests are seriously damaged and fruit trees are destroyed.

Four. The *Deuteromycetes* (du-tero-my-CEE-teez)
or *Fungi Imperfecti*

This class contains those fungi which do not fit into any of the others. Their method of reproduction is the most primitive. The spore grows into a new fungus all by itself. In other classes of fungi a new plant is formed only when two different spores unite. This action is called sexual, although it is not very much like the sexual activity of higher plants or animals. This union is also described as the "perfect" stage of reproduction. Those fungi which do not have it are, therefore, called "imperfect."

"It is very likely, though, that the deuteromycetes are really members of other classes," says a scientist. "Many fungi are so small that it is hard to study them, even with the best microscopes. They may have a perfect stage that we have not yet seen. This keeps happening. All of a sudden we observe the union of two spores. And yesterday's deuteromycete becomes today's ascomycete."

There is yet another group of fungi that is very peculiar: The members seem to be plants, and yet they act a little bit like animals. After racking their brains, scientists decided to keep these in the plant kingdom among the

22

Thallophyta, and to put them all by themselves in a separate phylum or division. It is called the Phylum *Myxomycophyta* (mix-oh-my-KO-fi-ta). The members of this group are known as the slime molds, and they are indeed a slimy lot. They look like a formless mass of jelly and they move around very much the way an amoeba does. Whenever they come into the light, they slither off trying to escape. When they find something to eat, they flow around it and over it so that the food is just absorbed into the body. Many of the slime molds are colorless like jellyfish, but some come in beautiful shades of red, violet or orange. They are most often found in warm damp places, such as the humid tropical forests. Some of them cause plant diseases.

The story of the classification of these primitive plants does not end here. Sometimes fungi live out their lives in combination with other plants. When you look at the hard greenish crust on rocks or on dry ground, you are seeing one of nature's strangest and most useful partnerships. One member belongs to the fungi (usually an ascomycete) and the other to the algae (AL-jee). (I told you about these in my book, *The Wonders of Algae.**) The algae are very primitive plants, but unlike the fungi, they contain chlorophyll.

The combination is called lichen (LY-ken) and it can grow where nothing else can. The fungi help the algae to find and keep what little water is available. The algae perform photosynthesis and make their own food which they share with the fungi. Together, the partners can stand long periods of drought, freezing weather or incredible heat.

The Bible tells how the Israelites starving in the wil-

*New York: The John Day Company. 1961.

derness were given manna to eat. Since then, botanists have been trying to figure out just what plant manna might have been. Most of them now believe that it was lichen.

To this day, the plant is dried and eaten in parts of Lapland, Iceland and other countries when food is scarce. You probably would not like to add lichens to your diet. They are nourishing, but they have a bitter taste.

In addition to being eaten, there are a number of uses for lichen. Genuine Harris tweeds are woven from yarn dipped in dye made from lichen. In your science class you have probably used litmus paper in experiments. This paper turns red when something acid touches it, and blue when the substance is alkaline. Litmus, too, comes from lichen. This plant is also used in certain types of medicines and ointments, to thicken puddings and to stiffen some fabrics and papers.

By far the most important thing that lichens do is to make soil out of barren rock. First they weaken the stone; then they make it decay and break up until it turns into soil. Then it is ready for the seeds of higher plants to take root and grow.

Another unusual partnership arrangement exists between fungi and the roots of certain plants. If you have ever been to the seashore, you have surely noticed pine trees growing in the sand. You may have wondered how they could possibly live in such dry soil. They do so thanks to fungi which grow upon the roots. The mycelium can send miles of hyphae out in all directions reaching for life-giving water and minerals. It gives these to the tree, which responds by providing food for the fungi. This friendly partnership is known by the name of mycorhiza (my-ko-RY-za).

Lichen

Mycorhiza

25

Many shrubs and flowers also need this kind of help. The lovely orchid is dependent on the unlovely fungus which fastens onto its root. If you go into a hothouse where orchids are grown, the gardener will tell you that he always plants the seed in soil that contains bits of root taken from full-grown orchids.

Fungi and higher plants have lived together happily since the dawn of history. Students of ancient plant life have found that this partnership existed 350 million years ago. As the centuries passed, some of the higher plants involved in mycorhiza lost their chlorophyll. They did not need it, as the fungi on their roots gave them all the food they could use. By now these plants are completely helpless. Even when water and sunshine are plentiful, they cannot do anything. They depend upon the fungi for life itself.

3 ·

THE MOLD THAT CONQUERED DISEASE

A BULL GRAZING in the fields of a remote part of Yugoslavia flew into a rage one summer day. It did not like the looks of the man taking a shortcut through the meadow. The animal charged, stabbing the unlucky passerby with its sharp horns. The man, hurt and bleeding, managed to escape and stumbled toward the crude cottage where he lived. His wife, hearing his cries, ran out to help him. As soon as she saw what had happened, she dashed back into the house for a chunk of moldy bread. Without wasting a moment, she put the bread on the gaping wound. The man eventually recovered. Both husband and wife were convinced that the mold had saved him from infection.

This belief has been shared by many other people. Three thousand years ago the Chinese put moldy soybean curd on boils and other skin infections. Medicine men among the Indians of Central America used fungi to treat wounds. Primitive peoples placed warm earth, which contains molds and other fungi, on injuries.

As time passed, however, most well-informed men and women began to laugh at the idea that moldy food could be of any use at all. This was a superstition, much like Huckleberry Finn's belief that going to a graveyard at midnight with a dead cat would make warts disappear.

And yet in the early days of the twentieth century a doctor treating a sick boy remembered these old wives' tales and decided to feed the child moldy bread. The patient's temperature dropped and he began to recover. The doctor commented that if he were to tell other physicians about his method of treatment, they would think that he had gone crazy.

No doctor today advises sick people to eat moldy bread or wraps a piece of old toast in bandages, but now we can understand why these primitive remedies may have worked every once in a while. In fact, the idea that a mold can conquer disease seems a perfectly natural one to us.

This change in our thinking began on a September day in 1928 when a British bacteriologist named Alexander Fleming walked into his laboratory and discovered that one of the germ cultures he had been studying had gotten moldy. When he looked at this more carefully, he found that there were no germs at all in the part of the dish where the mold was growing. They had been killed.

Fleming wanted to find out how and why this had happened. With a carefully sterilized wire, he picked up a bit of the mold and put it into a test tube filled with a culture medium. This is what scientists call a liquid containing the nourishment a microbe, or tiny living organism,

Courtesy of Chas. Pfizer & Co., Inc.

The mold that gives us penicillin.

needs to grow. Soon Fleming had enough of this mold to study it under the microscope. There was nothing unusual about what he saw. It was one of the most common molds, a member of the Penicillium family. These molds grow in the soil, on bread, on cheese, on garbage. The spores float freely through the air, and one of them must have landed by chance on Fleming's culture.

This particular mold, *Penicillium notatum*, produced a chemical substance that was able to kill germs. Fleming named it "penicillin." As a test, he used it to cure an infected wound.

Even before Fleming's great discovery, the idea that good microbes could kill bad ones had occurred to research

29

workers. In 1877, the brilliant French scientists Louis Pasteur and Jules François Joubert had shown how certain bacteria or microbes can prevent the growth of others. At the turn of the century, two German researchers, Rudolf Emmerich and Oscar Low, discovered pyocyanase, an antibiotic produced by a bacteria. But they soon found that pyocyanase had a bad effect on humans as well as on germs. Penicillin, on the other hand, was able to destroy bacteria without damaging the patient (unless he was allergic to the drug).

In 1929 Fleming published a report of his discovery. And what do you think happened? It would be natural to think that he became famous overnight, that drug companies rushed to produce penicillin, that one terrible illness after another was cured. The sad fact is that no one paid any attention to Fleming's report. Scientists did not praise it; they did not attack it or say that it was wrong. They simply ignored it.

For ten years Fleming kept his culture alive and waited. And at last his moment came. In 1939 a group of scientists at Oxford University in England began a study of antibiotics. Fleming's report was read and research into penicillin began in earnest. The culture that Fleming had doggedly kept alive was put to use. You may have heard the names of the men who did this important work: Sir Howard W. Florey, Dr. Ernst B. Chain and Dr. Norman G. Heatley.

Soon they were ready to start experiments with the drug. Deadly germs were injected into eight white mice. Four of them were given shots of penicillin at three-hour intervals all day and all night. You can imagine how the researchers felt when they saw these mice recovering from

the illness, while the four mice that had not received the drug died. They tried the experiment again with 50 mice infected with streptococcus germs. Twenty-five of them got penicillin and 24 recovered. All of the other mice died.

The scientists were eager to try the drug on people, but they simply did not have enough of it. This may surprise you, as you have already read that the mold is so common. Unfortunately, it produces infinitesimal amounts of penicillin. Dr. Florey and his associates were able to get only one part of penicillin to every million parts of culture medium.

"You could get more gold out of ordinary seawater than penicillin out of the mold," one scientist described this sadly.

It was at just about this time that a London policeman

nicked himself while shaving. He did not pay much attention to this minor accident. But the days passed, and the cut did not heal. Blood poisoning set in. The policeman entered Radcliffe Hospital at Oxford and every possible treatment was tried. None of them worked. The man's temperature rose to 105°; his face was badly swollen; he was barely conscious.

The decision was made to try the new drug. Dr. Florey and Dr. Chain brought the tiny bit of penicillin which they had managed to gather. The policeman was given shots of the antibiotic at intervals of from two to three hours. The doctors waited and watched.

The first day passed. The patient was no better. The scientists were not discouraged. The fact that he was no worse was considered a good sign. During the second day the policeman began to improve. After five days of treatment, the impossible seemed to be happening: the patient was recovering. And then, disaster struck. The supply of penicillin was used up. The policeman died.

Soon after this a boy of fifteen became ill with a badly inflamed hip joint. His family watched with dismay as blood poisoning set in — a form of poisoning for which no cure was known. All hope of saving the boy was gone, unless penicillin could work. A little bit more of the precious drug had been made since the policeman's death. By itself this would not have been enough. But doctors had discovered that penicillin passes from the human body in the urine. They had, therefore, collected the policeman's urine and recovered penicillin from that. The injections began. Gradually the boy's temperature went down and the swellings disappeared. One morning he opened his eyes and asked for a few sips of soup. The penicillin had done its wonderful work.

"It was clear that this drug could save millions of lives, if only there were enough of it," says a doctor. "But World War II started in Europe in 1939, and the British could not devote time or industrial equipment to the job. The only place where this could be done, scientists realized, was in the United States."

In the summer of 1941 Dr. Florey came to this country, and the Americans and British worked on the new drug together. At first the mold was grown in glass bottles, each the size of a milk container. You can imagine what a slow business this was. It took about 100 bottles to produce enough penicillin for one patient for a day.

The scientists soon realized that they needed a more cooperative mold. A fungus family has many members. Perhaps the Penicillium group contained a better one. The hunt began. Researchers from the Department of Agriculture went to the markets and surprised shopkeepers by demanding rotten food. At last one day on a moldy cantaloupe picked up in a market in Peoria, the scientists found what they wanted. It was *Penicillium chrysogenum*, and it produced about 200 times as much penicillin as the old *Penicillium notatum*. This strain had some other advantages, too. The original mold could grow only on the very top of the culture medium. Its brother could grow at the bottom of the liquid as well, provided that air was forced through the medium.

The penicillium was taken out of the little bottles and put into huge vats about the height of a two-story building. Great stirring rods as big as ships' propellers were designed to churn the medium as if it were an enormous pot of soup. Cold water was run down the sides of the vats to keep the molds from cooking themselves to death.

Scientists were still not satisfied. They wanted the molds to produce more and yet more penicillin. If this was the best that nature had to offer, they would have to change nature. *Penicillium chrysogenum* was attacked with X rays and ultraviolet rays. Chemicals were added to the medium, and it was heated. In time a strain of the mold was developed that could produce more than 1,000 times as much penicillin as Fleming's original culture.

By 1945 enough penicillin was being produced to treat 7,000,000 patients. The wonder drug brought about cures in cases of pneumonia, scarlet fever, blood poisoning, meningitis, venereal diseases, diphtheria, tonsillitis, mastoiditis, streptococcus infections, rheumatic fever and many others.

The success of penicillin touched off one of the biggest searches in the history of medicine. After all, if the penicillium mold could produce a wonder drug, perhaps other microbes could do as well — or better.

A great pioneer in this research, Dr. Selman A. Waksman, came to America from Russia in 1910 with $40 in his pockets and a tremendous interest in soil microbes. His early work, though, was on the effect fungi and bacteria have on fertility, not on their possible medical uses. He actually recalls in his autobiography that in 1915 he found an organism called *Streptomyces griseus*, but did not test it to see if it could kill germs. Twenty-four years later when Dr. Florey and Dr. Chain were involved in their huge research program with penicillin, he began a systematic hunt for other antibiotics. He studied thousands and thousands of fungi and bacteria. And then in 1943 he discovered that

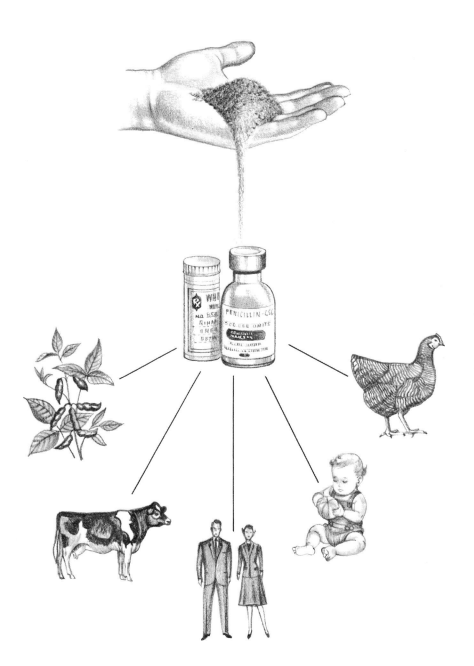

From a handful of dirt come antibiotics bringing health to man, animals and plants.

Streptomyces griseus produces an antibiotic that can kill such terrible germs as those causing tuberculosis and bubonic plague. You know this substance as streptomycin.

"Many people believe that streptomycin like penicillin comes from a fungus. This is not exactly correct," explains a scientist. "*Streptomyces griseus* is neither a fungus nor a bacteria. It belongs to a special group of organisms called actinomycetes. They are like fungi in some ways and like bacteria in others."

With the discovery of streptomycin following so closely on the heels of penicillin, the hunt for antibiotics went into high gear. Not a fungus, actinomycete or bacteria was safe from the searching scientist. A biology student who visited a research laboratory at that time reports that it was filled with hundreds of dishes covered with black or white or pink or orange fluff. These molds were not scorned as they would be if you found them on a loaf of bread or piece of fruit at home. They were the possible raw material for wonder drugs. Scientists experimented with every possible kind of mold and with hundreds of thousands of soil samples from all over the world. Chas. Pfizer & Co., one of the large manufacturers, built up a culture "library" of more than 20,000 samples. Laboratories asked school children, airline pilots, missionaries, travelers and explorers to send in little envelopes containing soil samples. Each one was tested.

If you like to perform scientific experiments, you can try the first test yourself. Take bits of soil from several different places in your garden or a nearby park and put each one in a dish together with a culture medium in which bacteria can grow. Commercial laboratories sell such mediums, or your science teacher can tell you how to make one. Leave the dishes at room temperature for several days to give the bacteria a chance to grow. Then take a good look at the dishes. In some of them you will see clear patches. These are the places where the bacteria have been killed by antibiotics produced by other organisms in the soil in the dish. The next step would be to find out more about the antibiotics. That is what the scientists at the laboratories did with many thousands of samples.

This great push paid off. During the next ten years most of the major antibiotics were discovered. In 1945 a kind of bacteria was found that could make bacitracin. A speck of soil from Venezuela yielded chloramphenicol, which you

The fading spoke in the wheel (lower right) means that the bacteria there are being killed by an antibiotic.

Courtesy of Chas. Pfizer & Co., Inc.

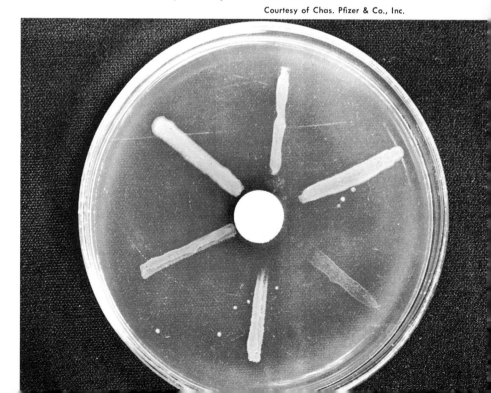

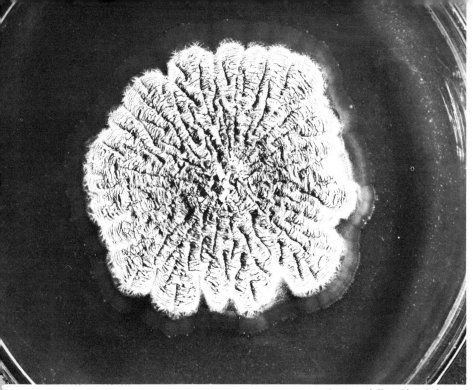

The mold that gives us "Terramycin."

know as "Chloromycetin." It can kill dread typhus and dysentery germs, as well as typhoid fever, whooping cough and Rocky Mountain spotted fever. In 1947, the year it was discovered, a typhus epidemic broke out in La Paz, Bolivia. All the "Chloromycetin" available was flown down there. It was given to 22 patients and they all recovered.

A three-year study of soil samples led to the discovery of "Aureomycin" in a drop of Missouri mud. A bit of earth from Indiana contained an organism called *Streptomyces rimosus*, which was able to produce "Terramycin." These two drugs are members of the "tetracycline" family of antibiotics, which also includes "Declomycin" and several other medicines. Researchers discovered erythromycin in Philippine soil and vancomycin in Indonesian mud. Another soil sample produced oleandomycin.

The discovery of penicillin set researchers on the road leading to the other wonder drugs. As a result, fungi are often given the credit for all the antibiotics. To be accurate, however, penicillin is the only really important antibiotic that is made from a fungus. Bacteria account for bacitracin and polymyxin. Practically all the others are produced by those in-between organisms, the actinomycetes.

As the years passed, scientists learned that antibiotics could do more than just kill germs. They help chickens, turkeys, pigs, calves, lambs, horses, dogs and minks to grow. The runts catch up with their stronger brothers. Farmers have noticed that chickens fed wonder drugs lay more eggs and cows give more milk. Radishes grown in soil containing penicillin weigh twice as much as usual.

Nowadays you will even find antibiotics on board whaling ships. The medicine is loaded into the head of the harpoon. When the whale is caught, the antibiotic enters his system. The entire huge carcass is kept in perfect condition during the long weeks when the fishing vessel is going home from the whaling expedition.

Antibiotics are valuable indeed. In the early 1960's, the police were called in to solve a bafflng crime. Cultures of antibiotics and formulas for making them were being stolen from a large drug manufacturer. Detectives discovered that test tubes were being smuggled out of the laboratory in the coat pockets of the thieves. The cultures and directions for making the drugs were then being sold abroad for hundreds of thousands of dollars.

4.

THE TINY DESTROYER

LONG AGO a twelve-year-old boy living on a farm caught a fox in his father's chicken house. The youngster had a streak of cruelty in him, and so he thought he would have a bit of fun with the captured animal. He tied straw to the fox's tail, set it on fire and then released the pain-maddened beast. As punishment, the gods destroyed the wheat crop with a disease that left the plants a reddish-brown color as if burned by fire.

That is how the ancient Romans explained the rust disease that ruined their crops. Each spring at the ceremony of Robigalia a procession marched through the city to a sacred grove where a yellow dog was sacrificed to the rust god, Robigus, and the Romans prayed to him to spare their grain.

The sacrifice, of course, was not effective in controlling the fungus that really caused the disease.

"Fungi have had a great effect on history," declares a mycologist. "Many reasons have been given for the decline of the Roman Empire. I think that we should add one more: fungi. The Empire was sinking from greatness during the first three centuries after the birth of Christ. We have reason to believe that these were particularly rainy years in the areas around the Mediterranean. The weather was favorable for rust, which surely brought famine and added to the Romans' troubles."

The history of other countries also tells of the harm that can be done by fungi. The weather was glorious in Ireland early in the summer of 1845. Then in July the temperature dropped and it began to rain. No one minded the stretch of bad weather too much.

"It is good for the crops," said the farmers.

The fields were green and beautiful. One morning in July a farmer walking through his potato fields noticed black spots on the leaves of a few of his potato plants. Within a few days the leaves and stems began to rot and an unpleasant odor hung over the field. In dismay he dug up some of his potatoes, and found that they too had black, rotten patches. He ran to some of the neighboring farms to ask his friends for help and advice. No one had any to give. Everyone else was just as alarmed by the sudden blight. It took barely a week for farmers to realize that disaster had struck. Field after field of potatoes was wiped out, as the disease spread over the entire country. At that time the Irish farmers grew only one crop — potatoes. If that failed, certain starvation lay ahead.

As the terrible, cool, damp summer drew to a close, not only the potatoes in the fields, but even those that had been picked and stored rotted. One family had put 60 barrels of

41

potatoes in a pit as a food supply for the next five months. You can imagine the despair when the parents went to the pit and found that barely one barrel of good potatoes remained.

Hundreds of thousands of people died of hunger and of the diseases that ravage undernourished people. Those who survived had only one thought: escape. They gathered their possessions and fled from their homeland. In a period of six years, the population of Ireland dropped from 8,500,000 to 6,550,000. Those who were not claimed by death had left the country. You have probably studied about the Irish Potato Famine in your American History class. Most of the Irish picked the United States as a haven.

The big wave of Irish immigration in the 1840's was caused by a fungus.

Ten years earlier when the potato blight was first noticed in England, several people blamed it on the new trains. Electricity given off by the locomotives was affecting the plants, they said. When the Irish potato crop was being wiped out, scientists devoted more time to a study of the disease. A number of them came up with the right answer: They blamed the blight on fungi. The name of the particular fungus involved is *Phytophthora infestans* and it is a phycomycete.

The troubles caused by plant diseases continued into the twentieth century. During the 1930's many Americans were poor and unable to find jobs. In 1935 an epidemic of stem rust, caused by a member of the basidiomycetes class, destroyed 135 million bushels of wheat in Minnesota, North Dakota and South Dakota. The results of this were felt throughout the country where business had been bad for several years. The farmers were wiped out; the railroads which had expected to earn money by carrying the wheat suffered as well; the people who had counted on selling fuel and equipment to the railroads lost out, too. None of them had money to spare for new cars, furniture, toys or clothing. The manufacturers of these products, therefore, went out of business. And so you can see how the trouble spread far beyond the original wheat fields.

Losses due to plant illnesses take place to this very day. Wheat is the most important crop of all. Agricultural experts have figured out that nearly one-half of the world's farmland is given over to wheat. The rusts eat up about one-tenth of the amount produced. More than 600 million bushels are taken out of the mouths of hungry people each year by the hungry fungi.

Other crops are attacked, too. In the United States alone, one-fifth of the oat crop is lost to disease each year. Trees are not immune either. At the start of this century, trees brought here from the Orient carried with them the sickness called the chestnut blight. By 1940 people had to look long and hard to find a single chestnut tree.

Just about every plant that exists can be damaged. Fungi are the most important single cause of plant disease. There are between 3,000 and 4,000 kinds of rusts, 1,500 different species of mildews, 900 of smuts. Among the rusts, more than 300 types infect wheat alone. Rusts fasten onto rye, oats, corn, pears, peaches, cherries, plums, pine trees, fir trees, hemlocks, fig trees, coffee trees, asparagus, beans, peas, beets and many, many others. Rots eat out the heart of trees. Smuts count barley, oats, wheat, rice, rye and sorghum among their victims. There is flax wilt and cotton wilt, cabbage yellow, leaf spot of sugar beets, potato blight and pear blight, downy mildew of lima beans, root and stem rot of soybeans, blue mold of spinach, apple scab and anthracnose of snap beans. The flowers in your garden are food for fungi, too. The botrytis blight strikes such lovely blooms as gladioli, lilies, peonies and tulips. Powdery mildews destroy the beauty of roses, lilacs, phlox, delphiniums and zinnias. Rusts appear on snapdragons, carnations, asters, chrysanthemums, roses and hollyhocks. Name a plant — any plant — and it has its fungus enemies.

Why are these illnesses so frequent? The reason lies in the makeup or structure of the fungi which you read about in the first two chapters of this book. You will recall that these simple little plants produce great numbers of spores which act like seeds. The fungi which cause plant disease are no exception.

"A single kernel of wheat that has been infected with the smut fungus holds from two to twelve million smut spores ready, willing and able to infect other plants," reports a farmer in Kansas.

Clouds of spores are so light that they can be carried on the wind for hundreds of miles. Rust epidemics can spread in less than two months from northern Mexico into Texas, then up through the United States into Canada. The disease leaps from Australia to New Zealand, from the plains of India into the high mountain areas.

"We have discovered some spores 2,900 miles away from the nearest possible source," states a plant pathologist. This is what men who study plant diseases are called. "You can see that to a fungus, the world does not seem very big."

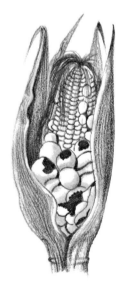

Spores do not need to depend on the wind alone. Insects carry them from one plant to the next, from one field to the next, from one state to the next, sometimes even from one country to the next. Twenty different kinds of insect carry spores of the pasmo disease of flax.

Rust fungi may not seem very attractive to you. Flies, however, find them irresistible. The rusts reproduce by the sexual union of two different kinds of spores. When the spores first appear, a brightly colored sweet fluid is given off. Flies cluster around and carry the spores to their mates.

Bark beetles spend the winter in trees dying of the Dutch elm disease. In the spring they venture cheerfully out into the sunshine, bearing the sticky fungus spores on their bodies. They settle on healthy trees, chewing into the bark to make their winter home. You can surely guess the end result.

"Birds are no help either," comments a botanist. "I caught a woodpecker one day and discovered that he was carrying more than 750,000 spores of chestnut blight fungi."

Rabbits, squirrels, rats and mice scurry over the countryside, taking large numbers of fungus spores along with them in their fur.

The spores of the fungi that make higher plants weak are very strong themselves. They can survive for years. Although the fungi need moisture in order to reproduce, the spores can live indefinitely without it. In the late nineteenth century, many different kinds of spores were collected and stored in a laboratory at the University of Minnesota. Sixty-four years later, scientists took these spores out and put them in a warm, damp place. Several of them promptly grew into new fungi.

What is more, the mycelium of young fungi can live

on in infected plants from one season to the next, even through subzero winters. The mycelium of the wheat smut, for example, enters the seed of the wheat and lies there quietly over the winter. When the seed is planted in the spring, the fungus starts to grow along with the plant. As the flowers of the wheat plant are formed, they are quickly transformed into ugly smut and can infect other plants in the field. Even if the seed is not planted the following spring, the fungi inside will not die. Wheat and barley seed were stored for seven years, and then planted. The smut grew again with the grain. Cotton seed held in storage for 13 years was not yet free of its powerful fungus parasite.

"Although it is true that fungi will not grow unless conditions are favorable, it is hard to find conditions that are not favorable to some kind of fungus," complains a farmer. "Warm weather is good for many of the rusts, cool weather for the blights. It seems that you can't win. The one kind of weather that discourages the disease-producing fungi is a long period of heat and dryness."

You have probably wondered why plants get sick. How do the fungi succeed in entering higher plants? These primitive organisms can take advantage of any weakness. If a plant has a cut or wound, the fungus can slip right in. The small hole bored into the bark of the tree by a woodpecker or by the claws of a squirrel is a huge open door to a fungus. The wind breaks off leaves, stems and branches; ice or snow cracks them. After a forest fire, the surviving trees and plants are open to fungus attack. Sometimes men become allies to the fungi without meaning to. In picking fruits and vegetables, we injure the plants that held them. Pruning the branches of trees leaves openings.

"As a matter of fact, whenever a leaf drops from a tree the place from which it fell is open to infection for a day or two," a plant pathologist states sadly.

Unfortunately, plants without any wounds at all are still in danger. All leaves have openings to the air through which they breathe out oxygen and breathe in carbon dioxide. These openings, which are called stomata, are so tiny that you cannot see them with the naked eye. Nonetheless, they are quite big enough for the fungi. The lower side of the grape leaf has about two million stomata. When the downy mildew lands there, it can get right into the leaf. Luckily, the stomata are not open all the time.

But even when they are closed, the plant is not safe. Some fungi can actually force their way through the unbroken surfaces of any part of a plant by means of pressure. It is as if they could walk through a wall. Some species have special outgrowths with which they can puncture the surface of a plant cell and so make their way in.

Once one kind of fungus gets in, it takes the attitude of "come on in, there's plenty for everyone." It weakens the plant so that other fungi can march in easily. When the apple scab organism enters an apple, it makes cracks in the skin. The pink rot fungus then has no trouble in joining its fellows inside the sweet juicy fruit. The powdery scab often opens the door for the potato blight.

Given all these facts, you might assume that plants are completely at the mercy of the marauding fungi. Luckily, this is not true. There are many weapons that can be used against these tiny but powerful enemies.

5·

GETTING THE BETTER OF FUNGI

"IF FUNGI were human, I'd say they have the will to live," complains a farmer. "They multiply at a fantastic rate; they sleep over the winter; they exist in the soil and in the air and in water; they find food in plants and animals — dead or alive — and in anything made from plants or animals. Small wonder that we have such trouble keeping them under control!"

What is more, they love to travel. The United States has not been invaded by a foreign army since the War of 1812. But we have certainly been invaded by foreign fungi. Detectives trying to discover the origin of plant diseases have traced 200 of them to seeds and seedlings sent here from other countries. To be fair, we have shipped many abroad ourselves.

If you have ever traveled, you have surely heard that ships are sometimes held in quarantine. This means that

Shipments of plants are stopped at the border.

they are not allowed into a country until officials have made sure that no one on board is sick. The same thing is done for plants. Shipments of plants are stopped at every border or harbor. If any are infected, they are destroyed. Unfortunately, this does not prevent disease from spreading over the globe. No one has yet thought of a way to quarantine the wind, which travels from state to state and from country to country, carrying spores with it as it goes. We must find additional ways of controlling plant diseases.

Name any method that you can think of and it has been tried. How about fighting fungi with fire? That sounds

50

drastic, but it works. Several years ago, some wheat fields in Mexico were attacked by smut. A nationwide epidemic was in the making. The authorities ordered that all the infected fields be burned out. At first the farmers objected violently, but they came to see that it was the only thing to do. The fire wiped out the epidemic with the wheat. People with small gardens are sometimes driven to the same lengths and burn their infected flowers.

Throughout history, battle after battle against fungi has been fought. In the Middle Ages the idea of discouraging fungi by means of a bad smell was suggested. When a branch fell off a tree, for example, the wood was painted with a mixture of ashes, cow dung and urine. By the middle of the eighteenth century, botanists were urging soaking seeds in purified urine.

In 1878, a compound made of copper sulphate, lime and water, known as Bordeaux mixture, was developed. The new product was sprayed on the vines where grapes were dying. It saved the grapes and the wine that was to be made from them. Bordeaux mixture became the first widely used "fungicide," meaning a chemical that kills fungi.

Since that time many other chemicals have been discovered. Large amounts are used today on plants, on seeds and in the soil itself. Insecticides to kill the insects carrying the fungus spores have also been brought into the fight against disease. These products are most effective in preventing horrible plant infections. Nevertheless, many people do not like them. The trouble with chemicals is that they are sometimes harmful to animals and men who feed on the plants. Other ways of controlling infection are being worked out. We are still unable, however, to do without

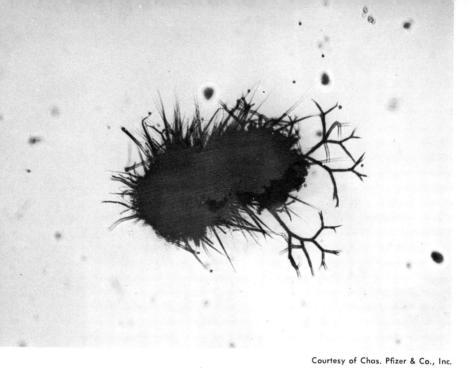

This mildew mold is young.

the fungicides, and so they must be used with extreme care.

"One way of cutting down on the amount that is used is to time the spraying carefully," advises an expert in plant disease. "The apple scab, for instance, drops eight billion spores under a single tree in a period of only 45 minutes. We do the spraying during that very time."

The Department of Agriculture has worked out a warning system to tell farmers exactly when to spray. It sends out "blight" or "mildew" forecasts. These are very much like the weather forecasts that you watch on television. The experts warn when the weather is favorable — to blight or mildew, that is, not to youngsters in summer camp. Eight to ten days of cool, damp weather . . . and the word goes out to the farmers to spray their fields.

If you talk with plant pathologists, you will find that they are excited about a whole new line of research. "We are discovering that certain chemicals do not kill the fungus at all; they just make it harmless. The idea is about the same as removing the sting from a bee."

The use of chemicals to control fungi is only one of many approaches to the problem. How many times have you caught a cold or the flu, while the boy sitting next to you did not? One of you is immune. The same thing happens to plants. Even during the terrible blight in Ireland, a few potatoes in each field escaped. Agricultural experts believe that it is possible to make every potato like the ones

The mold gets older and sturdier.

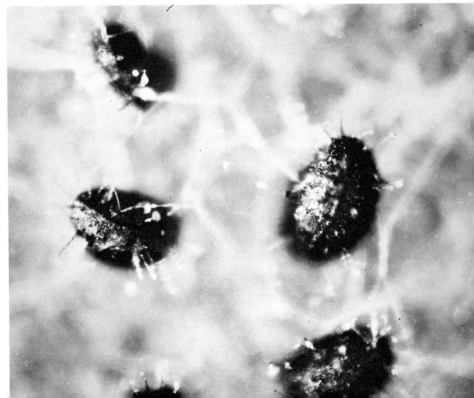

These oat plants must be combined to make one that will resist rust.

that escaped. This can be done in one way: breeding. Plants can be bred in roughly the same way as pedigreed animals. The breeder chooses a father plant that is able to resist infection and brings it together with a mother plant that can do the same thing.

Plant breeders all over the world cooperate in finding the best possible fathers and mothers. There are "rust nurseries" for testing wheat in 30 countries. Rice research stations can be found here, in the Philippines, Brazil, Thailand, India and Japan. More than 4,800 different oats have been collected from all over the world for use in tests. Wild plants are sometimes stronger than those grown on farms, so they are tested, too.

A few years ago the downy mildew covered the lima bean farms all over the eastern part of the United States. You might not consider this much of a loss, but the farmers and producers of frozen lima beans were in despair. Department of Agriculture workers combed the world in search of a resistant type. One was found in Guatemala and rushed here. Next time you eat lima beans, you will know whom to thank.

"Every so often we come across a plant family that has no immune members. We can search the world over, and come up with nothing," reports an agricultural scientist. "We do not give up even then. We try to *make* a plant that is disease-resistant. By treating it with chemicals or subjecting it to radiation, we can bring about great changes."

By today more than half of all the potatoes grown here are resistant to one or more diseases. Between 90 and 95 percent of all watermelons stand firm against wilt and anthracnose. Resistant oats have increased production of that grain from 27.1 bushels per acre in 1938 to 42.4 bushels in 1962. Before 1950, wheat was not grown in Mexico during the summer because of the danger of rust. Nowadays summer crops are harvested every year.

"The earlier work in developing disease-resistant plants was on a hit-or-miss basis. As they would say in television commercials, Plant A did not become infected with rust, and Plant B did. We would take the immune Plant A and use it for breeding purposes," explains an agricultural expert. "Today we are beginning to study just why it is that one plant is immune while another is not. This will eventually give us complete control of our breeding methods."

In 1960, three scientists working together made a dramatic discovery. They found that flax plants with a certain kind of protein in their cells are infected only by those rusts that contain the same kind of protein. The flax is immune to all other rusts. At some time in the future, a way may be found of changing the protein content of plant cells so as to make them resistant to the fungi that are eager to attack them.

With all this research, you might assume that you could stop worrying about plant diseases. After all, there are just so many plants. Unfortunately, there are not just so many disease-producing fungi. Breeders succeeded — or so they thought — in producing a variety of wheat that could resist the black stem rust. For a period of about seven years, farmers lived in a state of false security. And then all at once, the disease struck again. Thousands of acres of "resistant" wheat were wiped out. At first the scientists thought that they must have made a mistake in their breeding. But when they studied the rusts in the laboratory, they made a sad discovery. The wheat was still resistant to the *old* kind of rust. But a *new* kind of rust had developed, just a tiny bit different from the first. Work started over, and new wheat was bred to be resistant to the new rust. And again rust appeared that could ruin the wheat.

The reason why there are so many new races of fungi again lies in the nature of these tiny plants. More than 50 billion spores of rust are released on a single acre of infected wheat. By the law of averages, some of these will be slightly different from their brothers. The different ones are called mutants. With so many spores flying through the air, it is not surprising that enough of the mutants get together to form a new race.

"We are always running in competition with the fungi," sighs a Department of Agriculture official. "No matter how fast we run, we find that a new kind of fungus has dashed in to beat us. In 1944 we knew of 189 races of wheat rust. Today there are more than 300, and every season we watch for new ones."

There have even been laws against fungi. In 1660 the city government of Rouen in France ruled that all barberry bushes must be pulled up and destroyed. The keen eyes of the Frenchmen had observed that wherever these bushes grew, the wheat in nearby fields suffered from the rust disease.

The authorities could give no good reasons why killing barberry bushes prevented the rust, but it worked. As a matter of fact, it still works. Now we know why. Certain fungi need not one, but two higher plants to enable them to go through their entire reproduction process. The wheat rust spends a part of its life on the wheat plant and a part on the barberry bush. The blister rust that ruins the white pine travels between that tree and the currant or gooseberry bush. The red cedar rust needs the apple tree, too, if it is to live out its life successfully.

When you next hear farmers speak with hatred of the barberry, and see forest rangers look with loathing at the pretty currant or gooseberry, you will know why. Every summer the U. S. Forest Service recruits college boys to dig up and kill the bushes. This is a roundabout but successful way of ending fungus infections.

Some plants are beginning to take medicines the way you do. Antibiotics can perform their wonders on certain plant infections just as they do on human pneumonia or scarlet fever. A number of years ago, an antibiotic named actidione was discovered and tested for use on people. It turned out to be too dangerous for the human system. It

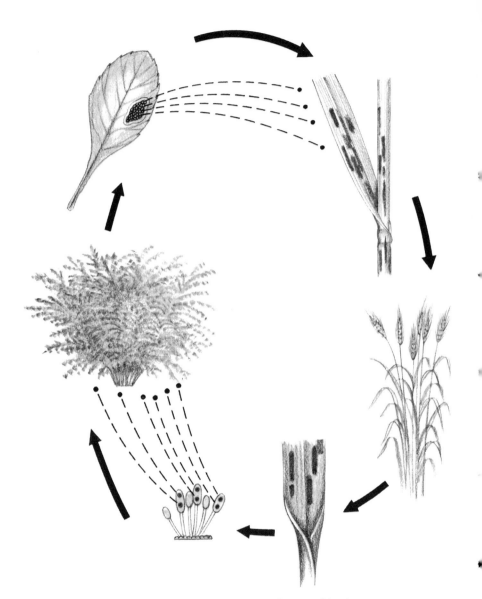

Rust travels from barberry to wheat and back.

was not, however, too poisonous for the system of the cherry tree or the bean plant or the rose or the pine. This antibiotic is now being used to control the blister rust that attacks the western white pine, and to cure several of the diseases that ruin lawns and flowers. Streptomycin, sometimes in combination with "Terramycin," helps some sick vegetables and fruits. Many other antibiotics and chemical compounds are now being tested and may become plant medicines.

Another system of controlling plant diseases has a strange sort of justice in it. This consists of turning fungi against one another. The *Cicinnobolus* fungus, for example, eats the spores of the powdery mildew. The *Chaetomium* fungus gives off chemical compounds that kill a number of its very harmful relatives.

Bacteria and other tiny organisms in the soil can also destroy fungi. Scientists at the U. S. Department of Agriculture are doing experiments in controlling the *Rhizoctonia solani* fungus which attacks more than 200 plants, causing root rot and other diseases. When oat, barley or wheat straw is placed in the soil, the harmful fungus is killed. No one is quite sure why this happens, but plant experts can make some good guesses. They believe that the presence of the straw encourages the growth of organisms that injure the Rhizoctonia. What is more, they use up the nitrogen that the fungus needs to grow, and release carbon dioxide which it cannot stand.

"Can you imagine anything better than preventing plant disease with something so common, cheap and harmless as straw?" asks a soil scientist.

Boiling water is another simple remedy. Unfortunately, not many plants can stand boiling. Seeds, however, can.

Loose smut of wheat is controlled by dipping wheat seeds in boiling water. A science teacher who grows his own vegetables says that he has held down plant diseases by treating the seeds himself. He puts them in a cheesecloth bag and soaks them in a kettle of boiling water for 25 minutes.

Good farming methods do not sound dramatic, but are essential in the battle against infection. In order to keep soil fertile, farmers have long been urged to practice crop rotation. They plant corn one year, for example, clover the next, and corn again the third. This method holds down disease, too. The fungi that infect one crop die out when another is planted.

Even after grains, fruits and vegetables are harvested, they are still the prey of the little organisms. Food packers figure that more than $500 million worth of food products are destroyed each year by molds and rots. One New York supermarket buyer reports that when he orders 25 carloads of fresh vegetables sent to him from Florida, at least one carload arrives spoiled and must be thrown away.

If you want to see how molds take over, just crush a piece of pear or a peach. Put it in a dish with a little water and keep it in a dark room for a few days. It will be covered with millions of molds. The same thing happens — a little more slowly — to whole fruit.

Refrigeration helps, but not enough. How many times have you gone to your refrigerator for an orange only to find a white or green mold growing on the chilled fruit? Store owners have the same problem. Many fruits and vegetables are, therefore, now being treated with fungicides or antibiotics.

You can see that the war against harmful fungi is being fought vigorously on all fronts.

6 ·

PLANTS CAN MAKE YOU SICK

ON A WARM April day not long ago, a doctor in a mid-western city was called to the bedside of a boy suffering with chills, high fever and a cough. He no sooner got back to his office than the phone rang again. It was another mother. Her son had the same symptoms as the first. This happened two more times that day. What was the connection among the four boys? There was only one. They were all members of a Boy Scout troop which had spent one Saturday afternoon clearing leaves in the city park.

The curious doctor checked the other Scouts. Sure enough, six of them were sick, too. A skin test revealed that all of the boys were infected with a fungus disease called histoplasmosis. The remaining 103 boys in the troop then agreed to take this test. The result was positive for 99 of these Scouts. This means that they had the disease, but in such a mild form that they had not known it.

Continuing with his detective work, the doctor tracked

61

down the source of infection. The fungus can often be found growing in the droppings of starlings, pigeons and other birds. Starlings nested in the city park. The boys must have breathed in the spores when raking the leaves that spring Saturday.

Even when birds are not involved, it is hard to escape the fungus spores. They are in the ground and in the air around you. In some parts of the country, the harmful ones are extremely plentiful. A woman was traveling by train through the Southwest. At one station she got off for a few minutes to catch a breath of air. That was enough. Ten days later her doctor diagnosed her symptoms as coccidioidomy-cosis (kok-sid-i-OI-doh-my-KOH-sis). A group of 14 people went on a two-day trip in the desert near the San Joaquin Valley in California. Seven of them came down with the disease.

Many people have never heard the name of either coccidioidomycosis or histoplasmosis. Nonetheless, these diseases are extremely common. In some parts of the country practically everybody has had one or the other. Histoplasmosis, which is found most often in the Midwest, has infected about 30 million people in the United States alone, according to recent estimates. The disease also exists in South and Central America, Africa and the Pacific Islands. Coccidioidomycosis is particularly frequent in the Southwest, where it has touched about 10 million people. This disease is seen in river valleys in other parts of the world, too. No one runs skin tests on animals, so we do not know exactly how many have been infected. But cattle, sheep, dogs and mice have been found that were suffering with these ailments.

You may wonder why so little is said or written about these illnesses, if so many people have them. The reason is that most of the victims blame their symptoms on a cold, or virus, or flu, or allergy. The disease goes away by itself without treatment.

That is what happens to the lucky ones, the people with natural resistance. It is quite a different story when the fungus attacks a person who is weakened by another illness or who simply cannot withstand the invading plant. Each of these infections has a severe form which strikes seldom but with deadly power. These diseases enter the lungs first, but they are not always content to stay there. The fungus can spread through the body, infecting practically any organ. This happens to one out of every thousand people who breathe in the spores responsible for coccidioidomycosis.

One young man spent several months being treated for tuberculosis, before it was discovered that a fungus was to blame for his trouble. He was not relieved to learn the correct diagnosis. A serious fungus infection is much more dangerous than tuberculosis.

Cryptococcosis (KRIP-to-kah-KOH-sis) sounds just as bad as it is. This infection is likely to settle in the central nervous system, which includes the spinal column and the brain. The fungus finds everything it likes to eat right there. South American blastomycosis, another usually fatal illness, has so far been found mostly in Brazil. North American blastomycosis is not quite so dangerous, but it is extremely unpleasant. The skin becomes infected in a particularly repulsive way. In spite of its name, this disease is found in Europe and other parts of the world, too.

You can sit next to a person with cryptococcosis or histoplasmosis without catching the illness from him. These fungus infections are very different from the measles and mumps. Each victim breathes in the deadly spores himself.

Fungi are not only in the air and soil, they are also always present in your body. Most of the time they do no harm. Every so often, something happens to make them flare up. This can happen when antibiotics such as penicillin or "Terramycin" are used to cure illnesses caused by bacteria. These wonder drugs not only fail to stop the fungi in their tracks, they actually help the little plants to grow. Bacteria are always in your system, even when you are well. They keep the fungi under control. Antibiotics not only destroy the disease-producing bacteria, but also those that were holding down the fungi. These then grow wildly

64

and cause illnesses. The most common one is moniliasis (mahn-i-LY-a-sis). This infection can appear in many different parts of the body. It most often brings stomach upsets or irritations in the mouth. In the years since antibiotics came into wide use, the number of moniliasis infections has increased sharply.

Another organism that normally rests quietly in the mouth can cause actinomycosis, if it enters the system. Even a tooth extraction may let the fungus loose. Luckily, this particular fungus is so much like a bacteria that it can be controlled with standard antibiotics. Cattle get a much more serious form of actinomycosis than people do. Farmers call this "lumpy jaw," which is what it looks like. Several years ago, scientists dug up the bones of an ancient rhinoceros. When they studied the jaw, they realized that this beast had been afflicted with the horrid ailment.

Some infections march into the body through a cut or a prick. A florist one summer was dismayed when his right hand became red and swollen and simply would not get better. He was amazed to learn that by pricking his finger with a thorn, he had made way for a fungus. The organism that was making the rosebud rot had infected his hand with sporotrichosis. A much worse infection called maduromycosis also enters the body through a cut. It is found in India and Africa and other parts of the world where people go barefoot. This one causes the foot and leg to become horribly deformed.

Over the years one treatment after another has been tried and given up in efforts to cure fungus diseases. These ailments are not like smallpox or polio. Vaccination does not prevent them. The great antibiotics, such as penicillin or streptomycin, make them worse if anything. Cer-

tain chemicals, the iodides, work against sporotrichosis, but not much else. The sulfonamide drugs have helped in some diseases and failed in many others.

And then in 1955 a group of scientists discovered a strange antibiotic in some soil taken from the banks of the Orinoco River in South America. It could not cure pneumonia or any illness caused by bacteria, but it was able to destroy fungi. Amphotericin B, as it was named, has done what nothing else could do. Before the discovery, doctors could not point to a single cure for cryptococcosis of the central nervous system. Amphotericin B was given to 69 patients who had this deadly disease. Fifteen were completely cured and 31 improved. People suffering with the severe forms of coccidioidomycosis, histoplasmosis and blastomycosis were cured by the drug.

Unfortunately, amphotericin B causes thoroughly unpleasant side reactions. It brings on fever, headaches, nausea and other difficulties. Treatment must be continued for weeks, often for months on end.

"We use it because we have to," says a doctor. "It will cure when nothing else will. But we don't really like it."

Another antibiotic that could cure these infections has also been discovered. You may have heard its name, nystatin, as it is prescribed for a number of less important fungus diseases. It can only be taken by mouth or spread as an ointment or powder. Although it could cure the major infections, it is not used for them. Nystatin produces such violent reactions that it cannot be injected into the system.

"The problem is that any drug strong enough to kill the organisms that cause the serious fungus diseases is likely to kill or harm the patient, too," says a doctor.

Less dramatic than these deadly illnesses, but much more common, are the skin infections. Some fungi can find nourishment on the skin, in the hair, even in the fingernails.

During World War II, more soldiers had to be sent home from the South Pacific because of skin infections than battle injuries. In a city in France in the early years of the twentieth century, it was customary to take children with ringworm of the scalp out of regular school and to put them in a separate school of their own. Teachers recall that the schools with infected children often had larger classes than the regular ones. More than half of all the men in the United States have had athlete's foot at least once in their lives.

Twenty different but closely related fungi are responsible for these nuisance infections. Some of them are very fussy. The one that causes ringworm of the scalp, for example, only likes children, and prefers boys to girls. The athlete's foot fungus picks on young men. Some of these organisms are patriotic and will only grow in their own countries. Two ringworm species are natives of Africa, and yet they are sometimes found on the American continent. Historians believe that they were brought here by slaves before the Civil War.

These skin infections can be passed from person to person, though not quite so easily as most people think. They can also be caught from animals. In farm country recently, 16 people came down with ringworm. It turned out that a herd of cattle on one of the farms in the area had the fungus. Children often get this infection from cats, and once in a while from dogs. One animal-loving veterinarian insists that the opposite is true and that more often children infect cats.

It is easier to catch ringworm than to get rid of it. Fungi are extremely persistant little plants.

"The infections on top of the skin can be cured with chemicals, such as acids, which peel off the skin together with the fungus. X rays do the job, too," states a doctor. "When the fungi get between the toes or fingers, we use preparations which dry the area. These organisms grow best when it is damp."

Infections beneath the skin are much harder to handle. The problem is how to get at the fungi. Injections of chemical compounds and X-ray treatments sometimes work. At other times, they do not.

You read in Chapter 5 how actidione, which was developed for human use, was turned over to plants. Exactly the opposite happened with the antibiotic griseofulvin.

This drug has a strange history. It was first discovered in 1939 and tested to see if it could kill bacteria. Griseofulvin failed the test, and so it was tossed aside. Several years later, researchers found that it was able to cure a number of plant diseases. Griseofulvin never quite lived up to its promise as a plant medicine, but by then scientists had learned one interesting thing about it: This strange antibiotic could kill fungi. Tests were run on guinea pigs infected with ringworm, and then on cattle and then on cats. All the animals were cured. The doctors moved on to human beings, with the same excellent results. This work was done in the late 1950's, 20 years after the first discovery of the drug.

"Griseofulvin is a very peculiar medicine," declares a doctor. "The patient drinks it, and is cured of infections on top of the skin and on the hair. It will not help against the serious fungus infections that are inside his body. Then, for some mysterious reason, griseofulvin works best on infections above the waist. The most dramatic cures are for ringworm of the scalp. The drug gets steadily less effective as you move down the body. By the time you reach the foot, it is not much good."

The battle against fungus diseases — big and small — still goes on. Chemicals as well as antibiotics are being tested. Another type of research is also under way.

"Many years ago, a number of people accidentally consumed cultures of a deadly fungus," recalls a doctor. "Sixty percent of them died; 20 percent did not get the infection at all. The remaining 20 percent got the illness in such a mild form that they had no symptoms. Why? When we know the answer to that question, we will be able to prevent fungus diseases."

69

7.

IN MEDICINE AND INDUSTRY

IN A SMALL French village in 1951 a strange epidemic took place. Men and women suddenly fell sick. Thirty of them became insane and had weird visions in which they believed that they were being chased by demons and snakes. To the relief of their families, they eventually did return to normal. Five of their neighbors were not so lucky; they died.

All of these people were afflicted with a disease called ergotism. They got it by eating bread which had been made out of rye infected with ergot. This is a fungus disease caused by *Claviceps purpurea*. Nowadays, we seldom hear about ergotism. Our bread is made much too carefully. During the Middle Ages, however, ergotism was very common, particularly among poor people. In those Dark Ages the grain was cleaned and separated into good and ergoty piles. The good grain was made into flour and bread for the nobility; the rest was left for the peasants. In one epidemic in the year 994, more than 40,000 people died. Hundreds of years later in the eighteenth century, the Russian ruler, Peter the Great, planned a huge battle against the Turks. He had to give up the idea when he discovered that his cavalry could not fight. The men were dying at the hands of another enemy: ergotism.

But fungi, as you have read, are seldom all evil. Ergot can also be used to make a drug which speeds the labor of childbirth and helps to control bleeding. A number of other medical substances come from the fungus, too. One of these has the odd name of lysergic acid.

On an April afternoon in 1943, Dr. Albert Hofmann, a chemist, was working with this chemical in a laboratory in Switzerland. By accident he must have swallowed a tiny bit. All at once, he began to feel strange. The table where he was working seemed unsteady. His laboratory assistants changed in size and shape before his eyes. Somehow he managed to get home. He lay down and strange visions appeared to him. Brilliantly colored scenes flashed across the walls and ceiling of his room. At last they went away and he was himself again.

His scientific curiosity was aroused. He had to be certain that the chemical was to blame. Dr. Hofmann went back to the laboratory and took some of the compound again. Sure enough, the visions returned. He set off for home on his bicycle. The trip was short, but the drug made him feel that every minute was a day or a year. The visions lasted for hours. For a part of the time, the chemist felt as if he were floating around outside of his body.

In this way the drug LSD-25 was discovered. It is being used in psychiatric research. When people who are well are given the drug, they act as if they were insane. For this reason, some doctors believe that experiments with it might tell them something about the causes of mental illness. Others say that LSD-25 is so strong that it is dangerous to use it at all. Only the future will tell if this drug can help us to understand and treat the sick. If it does, ergot will be known as the fungus that could both drive people insane and cure them.

It was also in ergot that a most unusual compound was first discovered. It was named ergosterol. When it is exposed to light, it forms vitamin D. This is the vitamin which is needed to make strong bones and teeth. In time, chemists learned that ergot was not the best source of ergosterol. Instead, they turned to other fungi, the yeasts.

Those tiny organisms give us many other important vitamins, too. In 1897 a doctor named Christian Eijkman was working in the Dutch East Indies where the illness beriberi was very common. At that time most physicians believed that all diseases were caused by germs. Dr. Eijkman had a different idea. The natives of the Indies lived on a diet that consisted of polished rice for breakfast, polished rice for lunch and once again for dinner. The doctor fed chickens on this rice and nothing else. The birds soon developed beriberi. This meant that the illness was not caused by bacteria, but by poor diet. Further research showed that beriberi could be prevented by taking thiamine or vitamin B-1. Yeasts contain large amounts of this valuable vitamin.

In the old days when a young man went to sea, one of the greatest dangers that he faced was scurvy. Eventually, naval physicians realized that this sickness was a result of a lack of fresh fruits and vegetables which contain vitamin C or ascorbic acid. British sailors were given lime juice

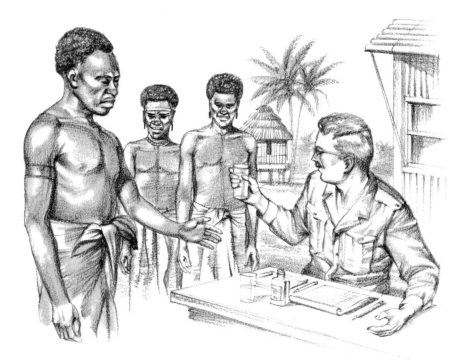

to fill this need. Landlubbers need a good deal of vitamin C, too. Yeasts contain even more than lime juice.

Folic acid prevents anemia, a disease affecting the blood; niacin keeps away pellagra, a horrible illness that can cause death. Both of these are vitamins in the B group and are available in yeasts. A look at the label on a bottle of multiple vitamins will give you an idea of the others needed for good health. Yeasts can supply many of these, including riboflavin, vitamin B-6, pantothenic acid and vitamin B-12.

Yeasts are such storehouses of good health that research doctors wonder whether they might prevent or cure cancer. Reports have trickled in about members of the African Bantu tribe, who have a great many cancers of the

73

liver. These tribesmen also suffer from malnutrition and vitamin shortages. It has not been possible to perform tests with these Africans. The doctors have had to content themselves with trying out their theories on animals. Rats were fed yeast and efforts were made to give them cancer. They did not develop the dread disease. Other experiments, though, did not back up these findings. Use of yeasts in the fight against cancer still remains a possibility for the future.

"We are also doing research with yeasts to treat skin diseases and to help in diabetes, an illness in which the patient cannot digest sugar," reports a doctor. "A compound named glutathione, which is made from yeast, appears to be useful in the treatment of radiation sickness."

The sufferings of people with arthritis, skin diseases, asthma and eye ailments have been very much relieved since the day in 1948 when doctors began to use a new drug, cortisone. Unfortunately, this medicine was terribly hard — and very expensive — to make. To add to the problems, cortisone has some most unpleasant aftereffects.

"We decided that we would have to make some changes in the nature of cortisone," says a chemist. "Fungi managed to do the trick for us. By adding these tiny organisms to the culture medium in which the cortisone was being made, we were able to produce two new wonder drugs: hydrocortisone and prednisolone. These are more powerful than cortisone and have fewer side effects."

Not only patients, but policemen as well find fungi helpful. Did you ever think that a fungus could be used to trap a murderer? Imagine the situation in which a man dies, leaving a large sum of money to a cousin. The police are suspicious. Did the rich person really just get sick and die, or was he helped out of this world? A sample of the contents of his stomach is sent to the police laboratory.

There it is placed in a test tube together with a mold. The detectives stand nearby and sniff. Sure enough, a smell that is something like garlic rises from the test tube. This odor proves that there was arsenic in the stomach contents. The detectives know that murder has been done.

Although mystery story writers might not be as interested, another important job done by fungi is that of making plants grow bigger. One of the Fungi Imperfecti produces a compound called giberellin that has this effect on plants. Like ergot and many others, this fungus was originally known for the harm it could do. In 1898 in Japan rice farmers first saw a new plant disease which they named *bakanae-byo*. It had a very strange effect on the infected rice seedlings. They became frail and weak, but they grew taller and taller and taller until they towered on their thin stems far above the healthy plants. Nearly 30 years later, scientists found that a culture of the fungus that caused the disease makes plants grow taller.

Many other compounds, chemicals, drugs and food products can be gotten from fungi. When you take a bite of a chocolate with a soft, creamy center, you probably do not think that fungi have anything to do with your pleasure. And yet the agreeable texture of the candy is produced by a compound called an enzyme, which is made from yeast. Enzymes are substances that help chemical reactions of many different types to take place. One of them keeps the sugar in the cream center of the candy from getting hard. Another softens animal hides, so that leather can be made out of them. For many years it was customary to put animal skins into a liquid containing dung from dogs or birds. The skins would come out soft and ready for tanning. About 60 years ago, chemists proved that the change was brought about by enzymes produced by the organisms in the dung. Since then leathermakers have been using the enzymes instead of the unpleasant liquid.

You can find an enzyme to do almost anything. One enzyme stiffens cotton fibers so that they can be woven on a loom; another then removes the stiffening to make the fabric soft. Some enzymes make meat tender, while others digest the starch from grain so that it can be used to produce beer.

The tangy flavor of many soft drinks comes from citric acid. This can be made from lemons, but seldom is. It is much more economical to get citric acid from the fungus *Aspergillus niger*. More than 40 other acids can also be made by fungi. One of these, itaconic acid, is used in producing plastics.

Glycerine is a chemical needed in the making of nitroglycerine, synthetic rubber and antifreeze. It also causes medicines to become sweet and syrupy. Glycerine is usually produced from fats, but it does not need to be. During the first World War, Germany was running out of fats. The military leaders wondered how they would get along without nitroglycerine to use in explosives. Scientists then recalled that many years earlier Louis Pasteur had shown that yeasts could be made to produce glycerine. With the help of these fungi, thousands of tons of nitroglycerine were made. Germany was able to continue fighting the war. This is one of the saddest examples of the use, or misuse, of yeasts.

Industrial alcohol (sometimes called ethyl alcohol), one of the most useful of all chemicals, can also be made by yeasts, although nowadays it is usually made from petroleum. When yeasts are used, they are added to a liquid containing a sugar or starch. Blackstrap molasses, a cheap by-product of the sugar industry, or wastes from woodpulp or grains provide this.

"I could talk for an hour on what industrial alcohol is used for," says one of the manufacturers. "It is needed to make plastics, polishes, synthetic rubber, soap, dyes, ether, medicines, paints, varnishes, synthetic leather, antiseptics, antifreeze, explosives, a large number of chemicals and . . ."

Ethyl alcohol can also be used to make a motor fuel. At the present time this is quite unnecessary. We have plenty of petroleum for gas and oil. At some time in the future, our descendants may use up our supplies of petroleum. The lowly yeasts may then be needed to keep the cars going and the airplanes flying.

The world of the future may be changed by the dis-

A test tube filled with *Aspergillus niger,* which is used to make citric acid.

Courtesy of Chas. Pfizer & Co., Inc.

This test tube holds *Aspergillus flavus*, which makes wine and chemicals.

Courtesy of Chas. Pfizer & Co., Inc.

covery of just how heredity works. What makes a person smart or stupid, handsome or ugly, healthy or sickly, male or female? Each characteristic is controlled by a gene, a tiny body inside the living cell. But how does the gene do its work? The fungi have been helping scientists to find the answer to this question.

The red bread mold, *Neurospora crassa,* is a very primitive fungus. It is easy for a scientist to watch it reproduce, grow and reproduce again. That is why it was picked in 1941 for use in experiments by Dr. George W. Beadle, a professor at Stanford University in California, and a young graduate student named Edward L. Tatum. The mold grows in a certain kind of culture medium and produces proteins, fats, enzymes and vitamins. The scientists bombarded the fungus with X rays and produced mutants.

78

Each group of mutants lacked only a single gene. This was enough to make them act differently. One group of mutants could no longer produce vitamin B-6; another could not make a part of vitamin B-1; a third could no longer grow in the original culture medium. In other words, a single gene is responsible for a single chemical reaction that takes place in the cell. This work led to many great discoveries about heredity.

Scientists went on to learn that the genes are directed by a chemical inside the cell. This is known as DNA, an abbreviation of deoxyribonucleic acid. The orders given by the DNA are carried to other parts of the cell by another chemical, RNA, or ribonucleic acid. These chemicals determine every single one of the hundreds of thousands of minute differences between people, animals and plants. A great many organisms — not all of them fungi — have been used in the research. Scientists report that yeasts are an excellent source of RNA.

Someday men may be able to control heredity. By making changes in the DNA, people could decide whether a child would be a boy or a girl. They could also make sure that a youngster would be bright, tall and strong. Drugs that change the DNA might prevent such illnesses as cancer and anemia.

All of this is far in the future, to be sure. Scientists are now hard at work attempting to produce DNA in the laboratory. As this chemical can start the life processes in a cell, this means that they are trying to create life. When man succeeds in this incredible accomplishment, you will know that the fungi gave a helping hand.

8 ·

EATING AND DRINKING

A LUMP of dough turns into a light, fluffy loaf of bread. The juice pressed from grapes is transformed into wine. An unappetizing liquid made of mashed grain becomes beer. Bread is very different from wine or beer, but all are made by the same tiny organisms . . . the yeasts.

Fermentation is the name given to the process in which yeasts change sugars or starches into alcohol and carbon dioxide. In producing wine or beer, the alcohol is the important thing. In baking bread, it is carbon dioxide. When the dough gets warm, the yeasts grow and break up the starch that is in the flour. Carbon dioxide is released. The gas pushes its way up through the dough and makes it rise.

If you bake bread or rolls at home, you are really performing a scientific experiment. You are observing fungi at work.

Bread was probably first made by chance. Men crushed acorns, beechnuts, wheat or barley kernels, mixed them with water to make a flat cake and then baked them. Yeasts carried on the wind must have landed on the dough. It was quite a surprise to the bakers to discover a light, soft loaf of bread coming out of the oven, instead of the thin, hard cracker they usually got.

The early Egyptians were the first to take advantage of this accident of nature. They made their dough out of flour and water and then left it to stand in the warm air until it rose. Before baking, they took a little of the dough containing the yeast and kept it for the next time. In this way, they could be sure the dough would rise again.

Thousands of years later trappers and prospectors in our Far West did the same thing. They saved what they called "sourdough," so as to be able to bake their own bread in the wilderness. The sourdough bread tasted very good. If you live near San Francisco, you probably eat it often, even though bakeries with supplies of fresh yeast are all around you.

In a modern bread factory, the unbaked dough covering barely one-quarter of the loaf-shaped pan goes into a steam box where it stays for 28 minutes. The warmth makes the yeasts grow vigorously. The dough rises until it fills the entire pan. It is then ready to go into the oven. The bread that comes out is usually good. Even if it were not, the bakers would not be treated as they were in ancient Persia. A law was passed there: Any baker who gave short weight or added straw to the bread would be baked in his own oven. That is how strongly the Persians felt about the "staff of life."

A modern bread factory.

Many primitive peoples reacted violently to anything having to do with bread. The rising of the dough seemed so mysterious that superstitions grew up around it. When someone died, for example, the family would rush to throw away any dough that was left in the house. The neighbors would do the same. The belief was that the angel of death had plunged his sword into the dough.

The transformation of fruit juice into wine seemed just as miraculous to the ancients. The Egyptians believed that fermentation was a gift of the god Osiris. The Greeks gave the credit to their god, Dionysus. People who lived thousands of years ago tried fermenting almost anything they had handy. They made beer or wine out of berries, grapes, grasses, roots, honey, dates, pine cones, cactus, grain, even out of fish.

The tribesmen of Central Asia fermented the milk of their camels or horses and made a drink they called kumiss. In the Balkans, cows' milk was fermented to make yoghurt. In China and Japan, the fungi did their work on soybeans and soy sauce was the result. You pour it on chow mein when you go to a Chinese restaurant. By adding molds to steamed rice, the Orientals produced a wine known as sake.

The Romans shipped wine to their colonies. Several years ago, a group of French scientists headed by Captain Jacques-Yves Cousteau recovered a Roman ship that had been sunk in the year 230 B.C. in the harbor of Marseilles. In the hold they found some bottles of wine stamped with the name Titus Latium. The captain opened a bottle and tasted the wine. It was not delicious, but it did not make him sick. After 2,000 years under water, that is pretty good for a bottle of wine.

As the centuries passed, wine making became more important. Great vineyards were cultivated in France, Italy, Germany and later in America. The grapevines were, and still are, forced to grow close to the ground. After a rainfall the grapes are covered with yeast cells. These are not lost when the grapes are processed into juice. They stay on and make wine. The yeasts in one vineyard are not the same as those in another. That is one of the reasons why French wine tastes different from German or Italian, even when the same kinds of grapes are used.

Although men have been making wine and baking bread for thousands of years, the part played by yeasts was not discovered until the nineteenth century. Before then people would have been horrified at the very idea that fermentation was caused by living organisms. They would have reacted in much the way you would if you were told that your favorite dish was made by worms or spiders. In the 1680's Anton van Leeuwenhoek invented the microscope and saw yeasts for the first time. He did not, however, realize what they were. About 125 years later a French scientist named Louis J. Thénard declared that the yeasts used to make wine were alive. Nobody at the time paid any attention to him. It was left for Louis Pasteur to prove beyond a doubt that yeasts are living organisms and that they are responsible for fermentation. It may seem surprising to you that a man whose reputation is based on his work with bacteria devoted time to studies on alcohol. Pasteur, however, was a professor at the University of Lisle, a city in France where wines and beer are made. His early work on fermentation started him on the research that eventually produced his great medical discoveries.

The new knowledge about yeasts brought about the realization that cultures of particular strains could be made in the laboratory. A single cell of the yeast can be picked out under a special microscope and planted in a test tube.

"By using a culture of the yeast that grows naturally in France," says an American wine maker, "we can make a very similar wine right here. Cultures are also necessary in dry seasons when yeasts do not grow well on the vines."

Chemists have learned to make cultures to order. For whiskey they select strains that produce particularly large amounts of alcohol. For beer they pick those that provide a big head of foam.

Beer drinkers do not always insist on just the right strain of yeast. The sun never shines during the six-month-long winter in the Antarctic. During a cold, hard winter in the early 1960's, the men at a research station two miles away from the main base at the South Pole ran out of beer. Although their shelter was tunneled 30 feet beneath the snow, they decided to make some beer themselves. What could they use for yeast? Their underground kitchen was well stocked. They promptly commandeered the yeast that the cook was about to use to make bread.

This is actually a switch on the old method of making bread. Bakers used to get their yeast from brewers who usually had quite a lot left over after making beer. Brewers' yeast did make the bread rise, but it had quite a number of drawbacks. The bread often turned out to be sour and unpleasant-tasting. The brewers also sent yeasts that were partly dissolved in liquid. This made the dough too runny. In the middle of the nineteenth century, a process was developed to press yeasts into a cake. This was much easier for the bakers to handle. In time, special strains were found that were particularly good for bread. These are known as bakers' yeast. Today in bread factories bakers work with yeast that has been processed into 50-pound cakes. These cakes must be kept in a refrigerator or they will start to grow.

If you bake at home, you probably use small cakes of this kind or packages of "active dry" yeast. This is compressed yeast that has been dried some more and powdered. The cells are still alive. In this form, however, they cannot grow, even at room temperature. They simply rest — for days, weeks or months — until they are mixed with warm water.

In addition to bread, the fermentation process brings us many other useful foods, medicines and chemicals. You have probably figured out by now that the industrial alcohol described in the last chapter is made in the same way as the alcohol for wine or whiskey. Glycerine, vitamins and citric acid are by-products of fermentation. This means that they are extras that appear when yeasts are at work. Almost all the important antibiotics are also made by fermentation.

Another product made by yeasts is vinegar. If you look at the label on the bottle of vinegar in your kitchen cabinet, it probably says WINE VINEGAR. To understand the reason for this, you have to know how vinegar is made. First, apple or grape or some other sugary juice is fermented to make wine. Then another organism, acetobacter (a-SEET-oh-bak-ter), is added, and the wine is transformed into vinegar.

A number of students have made vinegar themselves. It is not very hard. You need to get blackstrap molasses at a grocery store. Add three cups of water to one cup of molasses. Break a package of compressed yeast into the mixture. Put it into a darkened room and leave it alone for several days. You will then be able to smell alcohol coming from the liquid. Wait for another two weeks and look again. Acetobacter that is usually floating freely in the air will have gotten to the "wine" and will have turned it into vinegar. It will not, however, have the flavor of the carefully prepared vinegar you buy in the store to use in salad dressing.

Fungi like to eat, and in turn are eaten. The yeasts get their nourishment from starch or sugar and make bread. The molds move in and eat the bread. Then we come and eat some of these molds. In the village of Roquefort in France, they tell a story about the molds. Many, many years ago a young shepherd boy took his flock out to graze

on the mountainside. All of a sudden, there was a terrible rainstorm. Looking around for shelter, he noticed the mouth of a huge cave and ran inside. When the rain stopped, the boy dashed out to gather his sheep, forgetting his lunch of bread and cheese in the cave.

Several weeks later he happened to come back to the same place. He wandered idly into the cave where he saw his lunch still sitting on a ledge. The bread had turned moldy and some of the mold had worked its way through the cheese as well. The young shepherd was about to throw the sandwich away, but he was so hungry that he decided to take just a tiny bite. To his amazement, he found that the cheese was simply delicious. You know it today as Roquefort.

If you look at a piece of Roquefort cheese, you will notice that veins of a blue-green color run through it. This is the mold *Penicillium roqueforti*, which gives the cheese its flavor. This mold belongs to the family that produces penicillin.

The cheese is still made in the 25 caves around Roquefort. Some of these caves go as far down into the mountain as a 12-story building would if you turned it upside down. Everyone in the village works at making the cheese. The children register for the jobs they will want when they get older. The mold is grown on bread, and is then dried into a powder which is sprinkled onto cheese made from sheep's milk. Sometimes the mold is pushed into the cheese with a needle.

When you buy Roquefort, you had better eat it quickly. The mold keeps on growing, even after the cheese has been packaged and sent to the market. The cheese makers know about this and allow time for it. But if the cheese is

Making a pure
Penicillium roqueforti mold.

not eaten within 60 days after its arrival in the United States, you can expect a very strong-tasting dish.

In America the *Penicillium roqueforti* mold is added to cheese made out of cows' or goats' milk. We call this "blue" cheese rather than Roquefort. If you want to see *Penicillium roqueforti* by itself, scrape a bit of the vein out of a piece of blue cheese. Put it on a piece of rye bread dampened with a few drops of milk. Keep this in a dark part of your kitchen for about a week. By then the bread will be covered by this one mold. You could take it to school and study it under a microscope.

Another member of the Penicillium group makes a cheese that is soft and runny inside. This cheese was once served to the Emperor Napoleon. He enjoyed it very much and asked what it was.

"Oh, it's just the cheese they make in the village of Camembert," he was told.

"Then that will be the name of the cheese," he replied.

The mold was named *Penicillium camemberti* after the village, too — but that was many years later. Like many other cheese eaters, Napoleon did not realize that a food can be improved by a humble mold.

9 ∙

FOOD OF THE FUTURE

WHEN YOUR great-great-grandchildren come in from playing ball and ask, "What's for dinner?" the answer might very well be "yeast stew" or "yeast 'n' beans."

This may seem hard to believe today when there are so many good things to eat. But it will not always be that way. The population of the world is growing so fast that unless the supply of food increases, too, the time will come when there simply will not be enough to go around. Three billion people are on the earth right now. By the year 2000 there will probably be six billion of us. All these men, women and children will need schools, factories and office buildings. These will take up so much room that there will be little land left for growing wheat, grazing cattle or raising chickens. The oceans will provide the families of the future with fish. Food will probably be made from algae, the one-celled plants that form the scum on top of stagnant ponds. But these will not be enough.

Your descendants may have to follow the example of some members of the animal kingdom in order to have enough to eat. Certain ants cultivate fungus gardens for their food. The workers chew up leaves and pack them into beds where the fungi can grow. Some of the gardens are big enough to produce food for more than half a million ants. Older ants put bits of the fungus into the mouth parts of the babies. When a queen goes out to found a new colony, she carries a little of the fungi with her so that a new garden can be started.

Termites like the tiny plants, too. Expectant mothers and infant termites are fed fungi, which contain the vitamins that help them to grow and be strong. Ambrosia beetles eat the spores of a fungus which grows on the walls of the tunnels that are their homes. This is the only item on the beetles' menu. The fungi provide them with all the food elements they need to live.

While men could not exist on a diet of just fungi, we too can get much of the nourishment we need from them. Some yeasts are half protein, the same energy source you find in meat.

The yeasts that may become a food of the future are different from the ones that make bread rise, and beer and wine ferment. They belong to a strain called *Torula utilis*. This strain was recently renamed *Candida utilis*, but the food yeast is still called by the old name of torula yeast. This type does not make alcohol and gives rather little carbon dioxide. It simply takes in nourishment and grows and grows and grows, producing one yeast cell after the other.

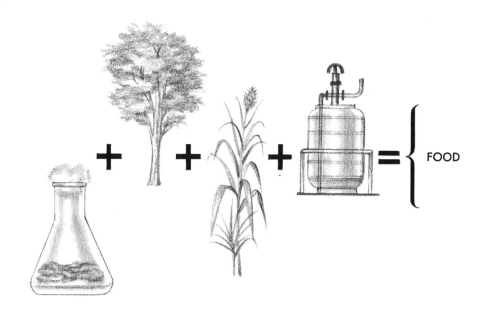

Yeasts become food.

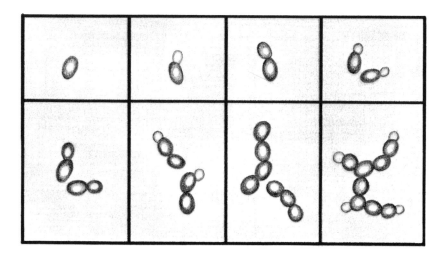

Yeast cells are multiplying.
(greatly enlarged)

Children in the years ahead could depend upon yeasts to give them the vim and vigor that you get from a juicy steak. The herds of cattle that provide us with beef occupy millions of acres. The yeasts can be grown in factories taking up a quarter of an acre of land apiece. More than 40 million tons of protein could be produced in this way on only 10,000 acres.

These yeasts make protein faster than any other plant or animal. Farmers have figured that a 1,000-pound steer gives less than a pound of beef for every day of the months it takes him to grow. Half a ton of soybean seed will produce 82 pounds of soybean meal for each day of the weeks that pass between planting and harvest. That is more than any other crop can do. But yeasts break that record easily. One thousand pounds of yeast reproduces itself so fast that it turns into 6,000 or 7,000 pounds of protein in a single day and night of factory production. In experiments, yeast has done even better. Scientists calculate that 1,000 pounds could grow into 100,000 pounds of protein in 24 hours, if production methods were improved.

Soybeans need land and fertilizer if they are to grow. Cattle, hogs and lambs must have hundreds of pounds of feed. As the population increases, animals will not be allowed to gobble up anything that might be boiled and flavored and made into food for humans. Yeasts, luckily, are so greedy that they will eat anything — so long as it contains starch or sugar. They can even get nourishment from products that you do not think of as food at all.

The idea of making food out of useless things came during World War I when many people in Europe were starving. The animals suffered first, as men and women ate the food that was formerly given to the beasts. Agricultural experts then got the idea of growing fungi on straw and feeding that to cattle. This provided the cows and bulls with some of the protein they needed. Then an attempt was made to turn wood into food for people. The early experiments, which were made in Germany, were not too successful. As soon as wheat and rye and beef and chicken were available, everyone breathed a sigh of relief and went back to eating them.

Unfortunately, it was only a matter of time before hunger struck again. Improved methods were worked out for producing food yeasts out of wood. By the end of World War II, six factories were making yeast in this way in Germany. In a single year, 15,000 tons of it were eaten. During the fighting, the torula culture at one of the factories was spilled. The chemists swept up the mess on the floor and put it all into a big vat. Enough of the yeast was left in it to start the process going again.

You may be wondering why anyone would want to use up valuable trees to make food. After all, we need wood for building, for fuel, for making paper, rayon and many other extremely important things. In the future, every remaining tree will surely be even more valuable than it is today. The yeasts, however, will not take away one log of wood that could be used for anything else. They are perfectly content with the part of the wood that is thrown away when paper is made.

In this process, the log is cut up into small chips, placed in a huge pressure cooker and boiled. About half of the wood does not dissolve and turns into the pulp that is made into paper. The other half dissolves into a liquid and is usually discarded. The yeasts can grow in that waste liquid. Enough wood is left in it to provide them with the sugar they need. Although most people are not aware of it, all trees — not just maple trees — contain sugar. It does not always taste sweet and it usually cannot be digested by human beings, but nonetheless it is there. The only extra things the yeasts ask are plenty of air, a temperature of around 90° Fahrenheit, and a touch of nitrogen and a few other minerals.

It is quite possible that in the world of the future, all trees will be protected by the governments and saved for their beauty and the shade that they give. Plastics may be used instead of paper. The yeasts could then be grown on the wastes produced by the sugar industry. The fungi thrive in leftover crude cane-sugar solutions and in extra molasses. Even today, bakers' yeast is grown in molasses. In tropical countries there are huge sugar plantations. When most land is needed for housing, the remaining farms and plantations will have to do double duty. Factories making yeasts could be placed right on the plantations. A single acre of ground could then produce both five tons of sugar and two and a half tons of torula a year.

The British worked out a method of growing yeasts on molasses when food was scarce in World War II. A small experimental plant succeeded in turning out 240 pounds of dry yeast in 24 hours. After testing the yeast on rats, it was tried on humans. A group of 100 men in the Air Force received the fungi in stews, puddings and pie crusts. Biscuits containing this food yeast were then given to children who had been poorly fed during the bombings. The extra protein helped them to regain weight and energy.

Bigger copies of the British experimental plant were set up on sugar plantations in the British West Indies and in parts of Africa. Patients in a leper colony in Trinidad were suffering from malnutrition as well as from their terrible disease. When yeasts were added to their diet, they felt better. Prisoners in the Royal Gaol in Nigeria were in poor physical condition, and improved when given the fungi. In Central Africa torula has been added to a popular native dish prepared from flowers and leaves. In other parts of Africa where the people live on corn, it was slipped into the corn porridge or bread. In the many parts of the world where rice is the main course at every meal, people are short of energy. This difficulty can be solved by adding high-protein torula to the curry and spices used to give flavor to the rice.

During World War II, a group of Dutch prisoners of war in a Japanese prison camp in Java were starving. One of the hungry men suggested that they might try to grow their own food. The idea seemed impossible to carry out. There were no seeds to plant, and no way of getting any.

"The only thing that appears out of nowhere," one of them remarked, "is the mold which is blown on the wind and settles wherever it can find starch or sugar."

The other men listened and decided to grow yeasts which they could eat. The starch to feed the fungi came from old, rotten potatoes. As yeasts must have some nitrogen, the prisoners put bits of spoiled fish or meat into the broth where the organisms were growing. Sometimes there was no fish or meat of any kind. The desperate men then distilled their own urine and obtained ammonia, which contains nitrogen. With these crude supplies, they produced more than 130 pounds of food yeast a week, and saved themselves from starvation.

Even today in many parts of the world, people are going hungry. Children who are undernourished and do not get enough protein can develop an illness with the strange name of kwashiorkor. Many of them live in countries where their parents would be horrified by the very idea of serving meat or milk even if it were offered for nothing by charitable organizations. Religious customs forbid them to eat anything that comes from an animal. Doctors at the Institute of Nutrition of Central America and Panama, INCAP for short, realized recently that the only way to save these children was to develop a cheap food concentrate that was high in protein — and that was made out of plants. The poor people in Mexico and Central America live mostly on tortillas, which are flat cakes of a cornmeal dough called *masa*. The doctors decided to use masa in their mixture. They added dried sesame and cottonseed and kikuyu grass. To increase the amount of vitamins and protein, they used torula yeast. The mixture was named Incaparina, after the Institute. It was put into a double boiler and cooked with water and sugar. The children downed the sweet drink with pleasure, and the symptoms of kwashiorkor began to disappear.

Even people who are not starving can benefit from extra protein and vitamins. Some torula yeast is being eaten in the United States right now. You may have had some yourself without knowing it. Two large paper manufacturers are using their leftovers to produce about 8,000 tons a year. You can sometimes find torula listed on the labels of foods you see in the supermarket. The added yeast increases the food value of certain canned and frozen soups, barbecue sauces, pork and beans, canned and frozen vegetables, stews, gravies, cheese spreads, TV dinners, crackers, potato chips and baby foods. Your pet may get some torula, too. It is being put in the feed for dogs and cats, as well as for cattle, lambs, fish and minks.

You have probably noticed that the yeast is always added to something else. This is not done because of the taste. Torula has a rather pleasant nutty flavor. But tests made with rats have shown that too much of a good thing can be bad. When the animals got yeast as their only source of protein, they grew poorly and gave birth to extremely small babies. Other rats developed liver damage. It became clear that torula could never become the only dish for people to eat. It must be used as an extra food.

In addition to protein, the fungi cells contain between 2 and 6 percent of fat. By making changes in the culture medium in which the yeasts are grown, the amount of fat in the cell can be increased. In some tests the yeasts have become more than half fat. When all foods are scarce, therefore, it would be possible to grow some yeasts for protein and others for fats.

With the help of the yeasts, the world will be able to feed the hungry generations of the future.

The fungi may even provide food for our spacemen. Scientists are working on ways to grow molds on human wastes. These tiny organisms may appear on the menus served to men and women on spaceships, satellites or colonies on other planets.

10·

THE STORY OF MUSHROOMS

NEXT TIME you are in the country, walk with your eyes on the ground and you will discover some of the strangest plants in the world.

If you think that all mushrooms look like the ones you see in the supermarket, you are in for some surprises. That lump of jelly in a fallen log is a mushroom. The cap of a mushroom can be round, or shaped like a cone, saddle, trumpet or lily. It might remind you of the head of a bear, or an ear, or a clump of coral. You can find mushrooms that are red, or orange, or yellow, or green, or blue, or violet, or brown, or black, or tan, or white. The caps may be spotted or pitted or dotted or plain. The jack-o'-lantern mushroom glows in the night, casting an eerie light through the woods. (Do not eat this one.)

If you ever travel to distant lands, you will see even stranger sights. In Nigeria the "star" mushroom that attaches itself to palm trees twinkles brightly. The "monkey head" mushroom of China has a cap with yellow hair on it,

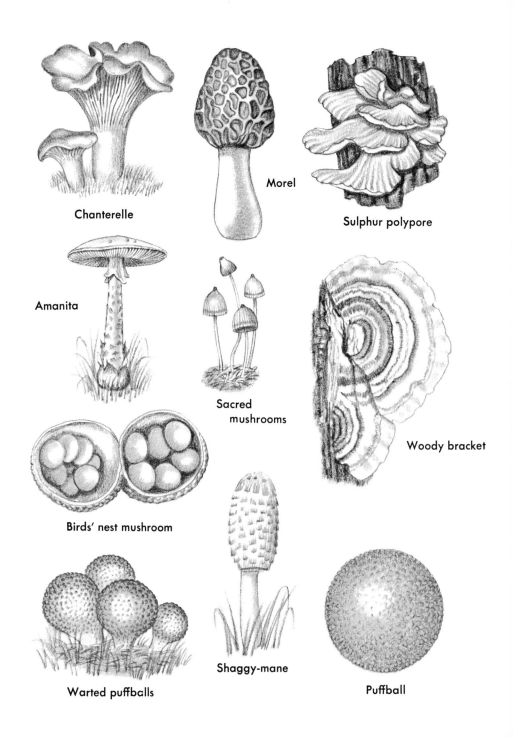

Chanterelle

Morel

Sulphur polypore

Amanita

Sacred
mushrooms

Woody bracket

Birds' nest mushroom

Warted puffballs

Shaggy-mane

Puffball

two dots for eyes and curves that look like a nose and mouth. The Chinese say that it is always in love. If you follow the direction of the "eyes," you will find that the "monkey head" is looking tenderly at another mushroom.

The odor of mushrooms varies as much as the appearance. It may be like soap or radishes, the chlorine of swimming pools, cod-liver oil, bitter almonds or rotten fish.

"Many wild mushrooms taste completely different from the ones served in most restaurants," says a man who spends his weekends searching the countryside for the fungi. "One is peppery; another is nutty. I have eaten mushrooms that reminded me of oysters, and others that were like a delicate breast of chicken or veal."

The mushroom family is so big that it includes all kinds of sisters, brothers and cousins. Three thousand species have been discovered in the Western Hemisphere alone. Not all of these are good to eat. In fact, so many are not safe that you should never sample a wild mushroom without first checking with an adult. Some people call any mushrooms which are not edible "toadstools." Mycologists do not like that term. They use the word "mushroom" for all of this group.

If you ever go searching for mushrooms, you may be lucky enough to find the morel with its spongy, pitted cap. Many people consider it to be the most delicious mushroom in the world. An old legend has it that one day the devil met an aged woman in the woods. He was in a terrible temper, so he grabbed her, tore her up into little pieces and scattered them. Wherever one of the pieces fell, a morel grew. This story was to explain why this mushroom is so hard to handle.

It will not even grow in captivity. You can find it in the spring, but never twice in the same place. Each year it shifts to new ground. The mushroom hunter who finds morels can make some money fast. An expensive restaurant recently paid $10 a pound. It is hard for the chef to get any, even at that price. The hunter is too often tempted to bring home the mushrooms and eat them himself. That is why so many us have never even tasted a morel.

The huge puffball that can be as big as a foot in diameter is often the reward of those who go on the mushroom hunt in fall. Puffballs may be eaten raw in salads, or breaded and fried like a veal cutlet. The shaggy-mane mushroom, which gets its name from the brownish tufts on its cap, must be cooked and eaten the day it is picked. The cap quickly dissolves into an inky-black fluid. When you have walked in the woods, you have surely seen the sulphur polypore. This mushroom consists of a series of shelves of yellow rosettes growing out from the sides of trees. It probably did not occur to you that it was a mushroom or that it could be eaten. The polypores are tasty when sautéed in butter. You see, a mushroom does not need to be pretty in order to be good.

When you eat mushrooms, you are following the example of people all over the world since the dawn of history. These fungi were among mankind's first foods. Primitive peoples believed that there was something supernatural about mushrooms. They could not understand how these plants could spring up suddenly overnight, or even after a brief rainstorm. You have surely seen a clump of little brown mushrooms jump up on your lawn after a summer rain. The ancients explained this by saying that mushrooms were produced by a bolt of lightning.

The true explanation seems almost as miraculous. What we call a mushroom is only the fruit part of the fungus. The rest of it, hidden beneath the ground, is the mycelium. That is the tangled mass of rootlike threads which forms the body of almost all fungi. The mycelium gathers in the nourishment until the mushroom (or fruit) is ready to sprout. All it needs is rainfall or a damp night to encourage it to push its way to the surface. The rising mushroom has so much force that it can break through pavement or sidewalk.

In most species a tiny white ball at last appears on the surface and begins to grow, rising onto a thin stem. The cap is held tight to the sides by a membrane. Then, all at once, it opens like an umbrella, tearing through the membrane. If you look at the underside of the cap, you will see spokes, known as gills. The spores or seeds are on the gills. The cap of the mushroom flattens gradually, and as it does, the spores fall to the ground. Each mushroom can release about a million spores a minute. These are frail; only one out of a billion survives and grows to form a new mycelium.

Some mushroom spores are white; others are yellow or pink or purple or brown or black. If you want to see this for yourself, make "spore prints" of as many different mushrooms as you can find. Take each mushroom and pull off the stem. Put the cap on a piece of paper, half white and half black, with the gills resting on the paper. Cover the mushroom with a glass into which you have put a tiny piece of wet cotton. In an hour or two, lift up the glass and the mushroom cap. Enough spores will have fallen onto the paper to make a print. You need the white half of the paper in case the spores are black, and the black in case the spores are white. If you spray the print with lacquer, you can keep it as a record. Just as no two people have the same fingerprints, no two species of mushrooms will give the same spore print.

Sometimes mushrooms grow in a huge, perfect circle.

You have probably heard this called a "fairy ring." The grass grows inside and outside the circle. The ring is bare, except for the mushrooms. This happens when a clump of mycelium grows beneath a large field or hillside. The mycelium spreads out in all directions looking for food. Mushrooms spring up at the outer edges of the circle. They use up the food in the ground around them, so the grass there dies. The mycelium then spreads out farther, looking for more food. The next year the mushrooms spring up around the edges of a bigger circle. The dead mycelium where the mushrooms grew the year before fertilizes the ground, and the grass grows there again, filling in the inside of the circle. Each year the mushrooms advance, forming bigger and bigger rings. Botanists have figured out how far the mushrooms move each year. With this as a basis, they have discovered that some fairy rings are about 400 years old. The circles remain perfect because they are so beautiful that even hungry mushroom hunters hate to destroy them for food.

Mushrooms are not the only fungi that can be eaten with delight. The ancients who thought that mushrooms are produced by lightning claimed that truffles are formed when the thunder roars. The two fungi have a lot in common: They both hate the sunshine, grow beneath the earth and are considered delicacies by those who appreciate the finest foods.

There are some differences, however. Almost all mushrooms are basidiomycetes; the truffles are ascomycetes. What is more, no part of a truffle ever sees the light of day at all — until it is picked and eaten. It lies three or four or more inches below the surface. You may wonder then how anyone finds it. In the desert the truffle pushes up the sand a little, so that it casts a shadow. The observant Bedouin

A truffle

Pigs hunt truffles.

sees it, digs up the fungus, roasts it and eats it with a little salt. If there are many truffles, he dries the extras and eats them later as his caravan crosses the desert wastes.

In the rest of the world, people do not find truffles at all; animals do. Goats, bears, deer, rabbits, squirrels and mice all love these fungi. As it is hard to make these wild animals do our bidding, truffle hunters rely on either dogs or pigs. One trained dog once broke loose from its master, jumped a hedge, crossed a field and dug up a truffle 100 yards away.

Most truffles are found in France and are hunted with pigs. The hunters treat the pigs as tenderly as if they were children. To keep the animals from getting tired, they are carried to the woods under the hunter's arm or in a wheelbarrow. When the pair reaches the wood, a long rope is

A mushroom "farm."

tied around the pig's neck and he is given his head. The
animal smells the truffle, runs to it, and starts rooting it out.
Then comes the hard part. The pig cannot be allowed to
eat the truffle. The hunter must rush to tie up the pig and
give him an acorn to keep him happy. Otherwise, the animal will refuse to go on searching for truffles. Then the
hunter digs up the fungus with a special spike.

Until the 1700's mushrooms, too, were gathered by
people hunting through woods and fields. Then French
farmers had the idea of growing mushrooms in limestone
caves near Paris. As caves are dark, cool and damp, they
are perfect places for mushrooms. You will find such cave-
farms to this very day not only in France, but also in Pennsylvania and Illinois. Some people raise small crops of
mushrooms in the cellars of their homes.

Nowadays most of these tasty fungi are grown in houses that have been specially designed for them. These houses have no windows. The mushrooms are grown on shelves that line the walls. When these fungi are grown in the summer, the houses are air-conditioned.

Mushrooms are used so much in French cooking that many people think of them as a French vegetable. Today, however, the United States produces more mushrooms than any other country in the world — about 165 million pounds a year. Two-thirds of these are grown in Pennsylvania. Our farmers plant only one kind of mushroom, *Agaricus campestris*.

In other parts of the world, people get much more variety in their mushroom diets. Twenty different kinds are grown in the French caves. In many European markets, shoppers have a choice of both wild and cultivated mushrooms. The Chinese enjoy a jellylike fungus they call *mu erh*. It is a wild mushroom, but they control its growth. Young oaks are cut into poles and put out of doors in a damp place until the mu erh fastens onto them. In Japan the *shii take* mushroom feeds on dead wood. Logs are soaked in water and holes are poked into them. Pieces of decayed wood are then put in. It takes two years for the shii take to fasten on and grow there. Like mushroom lovers the world over, the Japanese think them well worth the wait.

11 ·

STRANGE TALES

DO YOU LIKE to read detective stories? Have you ever seen a plot like this one? A man died suddenly as a result of eating poisoned mushrooms. A few weeks later there was another death from the same cause . . . and then another . . . and another. It seemed suspicious, but what could all these people have had in common? Gradually, a rumor began to spread. They had all died shortly after insuring their lives in favor of a neighbor.

This man calmly told the police that each victim had eaten dinner with him a few days before dying. Why not? These people were his friends; they often dined together. And it was only natural for them to leave him money. Did he serve mushrooms? asked the police. Of course; he had an excellent cook who prepared wild mushrooms gathered for him in the woods by a poor old man. Perhaps this peddler had make mistakes once in a while and put a poisonous mushroom into the basket. It was certainly not the host's fault.

When the old man was questioned, however, he admitted that the host had carefully described to him the poisonous mushroom, *Amanita phalloides*, and had ordered him to gather some every time one of the victims was invited to dinner.

This plot may seem a bit hard to believe, but it really happened in Paris in 1918. Some of the intended victims escaped, nevertheless. The old peddler sometimes did make mistakes and gathered harmless mushrooms which looked like the poisonous ones.

You need not be alarmed, though, when you are next served mushrooms. All mushrooms sold in the United States are grown on farms. You will never see a wild mushroom in a supermarket.

But what if you go mushroom hunting? How can you tell which mushrooms are poisonous?

"It is very hard for anyone who is not an expert to be sure of recognizing a poisonous mushroom. The best plan is to stick to a small group of safe mushrooms that are easy to identify, such as morels, shaggy-manes, puffballs and sulphur polypores," advises a mycologist. "Pictures of these can be found in handbooks about mushrooms. Nonetheless, children should always show a wild mushroom to an experienced grown-up before tasting it."

Many people still believe in the old superstition that a silver spoon will turn black if it is put in a pot where a poisonous mushroom is being cooked. This is simply untrue. The *Amanita phalloides* will leave your silverware gleaming. And it is so poisonous that one tiny piece is enough to bring on violent illness, and often death. The flavor gives no clue. Many victims have complimented the cook before they collapsed.

The *Amanita phalloides* is as beautiful as it is deadly.

Its round cap is a pale tan in the center and is white around the edges. The long and graceful stem narrows toward the top. You can recognize it — sometimes — by the cup around the base of the stem, the white spores and the white gills which are too short to reach the stem. It is easy to miss these signs, though. The cup may be buried beneath the earth, and the color of the cap varies, too. Several other members of the Amanita family are just as poisonous as phalloides. They range in color from brilliant crimson to pale green to orange to white. The lovely white *Amanita verna* is sometimes called the "Angel of Death."

Most poisonous mushrooms are not so terrible as the Amanita. They cause stomach upsets from which the victim recovers fairly quickly. The kind of poison in the fungus also varies from one species to the next. The Amanita's power lasts through cooking, freezing and drying. The poison of the jack-o'-lantern and of certain of the saddle-shaped mushrooms dissolves in cooking water. If that is thrown away, the mushrooms are safe. No one recommends that these be eaten anyway.

The newspapers recently ran a story about two families in Brooklyn who were given mushrooms by a kind friend who had spent the weekend in the country. Both families spent the next few days in the hospital. Luckily, these were not deadly mushrooms, and so the people recovered.

Mushrooms do not need to be poisonous in order to produce startling reactions. In Michigan a few years ago a middle-aged man picked and ate a wild mushroom. He woke up at night feeling dizzy and sick and called a doctor who sent him to the hospital. When he got there, he joyously announced that he was entering the Garden of Eden and there were angels all around him. Then he shuddered, certain that the devil had entered the room. These visions continued for several hours. At last they faded. The man got up again in perfect health and went to work.

This strange attack reminded doctors of the time a very dignified surgeon and his wife gathered and ate some mushrooms in the woods near their home. All at once they began to laugh and act silly. They lost their sense of time and balance. Things that were near them seemed to be far away. They, too, returned to normal in a few hours.

All mushrooms contain vitamins, minerals and protein. Perhaps some of them contain something else . . . strange, and hard to understand.

In ancient China the wise men wrote of the dangers of eating the mushroom that could cause the "disease of the dry laugh." The person who consumed it would go on laughing and laughing and laughing without stopping.

A traveler to the Kamchatka peninsula of Siberia in the early years of this century discovered that the natives there served a strange mushroom at their feasts. After eating it, they became wild and excited. They would laugh and cry and perform unbelievable feats of strength.

Turning to Scandinavia, scholars were struck by the number of legends about warriors who went "berserk." You have probably heard this word, which means to act wild and crazy. The expression gets its name from Berserk, an ancient hero of Norse mythology. He went into battle dressed only in a bearskin and was famous for his reckless courage. Between the ninth and twelfth centuries, fighters and murderers in Scandinavia were known as berserks. These berserks acted just like everybody else most of the time. Then they would decide to start a fight or a massacre. The folk tales describe how they would first be seized with fits of shivering. Then all at once, they would go into a rage

so violent that they would bite the edges of their shields
and would attack anyone they saw. Even their friends were
not safe from their fury. After several hours, the mood
would pass. The warriors would be left stupid and weak.

In the twelfth century a law was passed that anyone
who went berserk would be sent away from the country
for three years. From then on nobody went berserk any
more. Why? If they were truly insane, how could a law
change them? Today many historians believe that what
happened was that they ate the mushroom *Amanita mus-
caria.* This is a relative of the deadly Amanitas. It is sometimes called the "fly amanita," because it is supposed to kill
flies who feed on it. (Many botanists do not believe that it
does, however.)

A different type of mushroom is responsible for the
strange behavior of the Kuma tribe of New Guinea. Every

Indian wise woman prepares sacred mushrooms.

so often these natives are seized with the "mushroom madness." They become lightheaded and silly. The married women dance, although it is not considered proper among the Kuma. The men run around, chasing anyone who gets in their way and threatening him with their weapons. But they are not really violent. The children hide behind the huts and call out to the men, urging the excited grownups to come and catch them.

You do not need to travel quite so far from home to see primitive people who use mushrooms that produce unusual effects. They can still be found in Mexico and in Central America. The weird mushrooms have been eaten there for hundreds, possibly thousands, of years. When the Spanish landed in Mexico in the early sixteenth century,

114

they discovered that three kinds were being used. One of these caused the Indians to laugh and act giddy; another made them warlike; and still another was considered divine.

Just a few years ago, an American banker named R. Gordon Wasson and his wife, Valentina, journeyed into the interior of Mexico to see for themselves how the sacred mushrooms were being used. They went as far as they could by car. Then they went on by muleback, climbing for 11 hours up a mountain trail into the country of the Mazatec Indians. They learned that the Indians only speak the name of the divine mushroom in a whisper or make a gesture to describe it. There is a ritual or ceremony every time the mushrooms are eaten.

In this tribe, only the wise men or medicine men are considered fit to eat of the sacred fungi. If an Indian is sick, has lost something valuable or needs advice, he asks the wise man to eat the mushroom for him. The spirit within the mushroom speaks through the wise man and answers. There are other tribes, the Wassons discovered, where the sick person eats the mushroom himself.

The fungus will not cure, but it will tell the patient what is wrong with him and whether he will live or die. The mushroom not only advises and foretells the future, it also causes strange visions.

A wise woman agreed to let Mr. Wasson eat the mushrooms himself. The taste was unpleasant, he reports, something like rancid grease. The mushroom also gave a tickling sensation in the nose, the way ginger ale does. He lay down, and it was as if his soul had been taken out of his body. The walls of the room where he was lying vanished and glorious visions appeared before him. At first all he saw were geometric patterns in brilliant colors. Then they took shape and became huge buildings with columns and stone carvings. He looked at a bouquet of flowers that was lying on the table, and it turned into a chariot drawn by other-worldly creatures. Landscapes more beautiful than any he had seen on earth appeared before his eyes. He looked out upon a great desert with camel caravans traveling across to distant mountains. He saw flowing rivers and came to a beautiful land where a woman was standing in front of a cabin. Through it all he was conscious of a sense of deep joy, greater than any he had ever known. He felt as if he were touching another world and would soon understand what life really means. Then the visions faded.

When he returned to the United States, Mr. Wasson took with him a few of the mushrooms which had been dried. He ate them in the less romantic surroundings of his home in the city. The mushrooms had lost none of their power. The visions returned.

Primitive people believe the mushrooms produce visions because they are divine. We are not willing to accept a supernatural explanation. The strange mushrooms have been gathered and sent to laboratories for study. It was found that many of them are members of the Psilocybe species. Chemists eventually discovered that the ones which produce visions all contain the same chemical substance. They named it psilocybin.

This substance brings on reactions very much like those caused by LSD-25, which, you will recall, also comes from a fungus. When a normal person takes either one of these drugs, he behaves as if he were insane. Psilocybin, too, is therefore being used — with extreme care — by psychiatrists in their research into mental illness. The Indians would surely be surprised to hear of the use being made of their sacred mushrooms.

12.

OUT IN SPACE

"BLAST OFF!"

The rocket hurtles off the launching pad and starts on its trip into space.

You have probably heard those words and watched that event on television many times in the last few years. But the television cameras are not aimed at every rocket that takes off. They concentrate on the journeys of Alan B. Shepard, Jr., John H. Glenn, Jr., and the other daring astronauts. You are not given the chance to watch fungi on their way through the atmosphere.

And yet the trips taken by yeasts and molds are extremely important to the astronauts, and to you — because you too may someday be traveling beyond the earth's atmosphere. These primitive organisms are being used as if they were space guinea pigs.

What effects will space travel have on people not only

right away, but in the long run? Will radiation hurt the children who will someday be born to astronauts? We cannot afford to wait and see. Human life is too precious. Officials of the National Aeronautics and Space Administration (NASA) need information now, so as to decide how heavy a shield of protection must be put on a capsule or space suit.

"The lower forms of life cannot give us the full answer, of course," a scientist points out, "but they can provide us with valuable clues."

On one of these experimental journeys, a four-stage rocket, the Argo D-8, was blasted off into space. In the nose cone were instruments designed to discover how much radiation is in the atmosphere 1,180 miles up. Going along as a fellow passenger was the red bread mold, *Neurospora crassa*. This particular fungus was chosen because scientists had already studied the way it reproduces under normal conditions.

Ships in the U. S. First Fleet were waiting to recover the capsule containing the instruments and the molds. After three hours, it came down in the sea 1,200 miles downrange from the launch site. The capsule had been in the radiation zone for 26 minutes. The cylinders containing the fungi were put into a refrigerator on board ship, and the vessel then steamed into the harbor of San Diego, California, where a scientist was waiting nervously. He took the cylinders and brought them to the Florida State University Genetics Laboratories.

What had happened to the fungi during their trip on the rocket? Many of the cells which had been on the space voyage seemed to be dead. They responded, however, to efforts to revive them. When they were put into a culture medium which was particularly rich in nourishment, they came back to life.

The fate of the new cells produced by the returned Neurospora was not such a happy one. Many of them were hurt so that they could not grow in a normal way. Whenever an organism reproduces, some of the daughter cells are mutants — different from the rest. Scientists know exactly how many mutants Neurospora usually give. The space travelers produced a much larger number.

These experiments are still in an early stage. Many more fungi, yeasts and molds must take similar trips before scientists can say for certain that radiation was the cause of the mutants.

Some fungi are being sent up into space; others may be there already. There must be living things in parts of the universe outside of our own little globe. The earth is only one planet going around one star or sun. Astronomers believe that there are 10,000,000,000,000,000,000 stars in the universe that might have planets revolving around them. Surely on some of these, conditions like those on the earth must have occurred. We cannot believe that, with so many opportunities, life happened only once.

Perhaps some planets have people on them who are much more advanced than we are. This could not be true of the other planets in our own solar system. None of them has as good conditions for life as does the earth. When we journey to our moon and to neighboring planets, our greatest hope is that we will meet some lower forms of life.

For this reason, every inch of a rocket, capsule, spaceship and space suit must be carefully sterilized. We cannot take the risk of carrying our own fungi and bacteria to other planets.

"They might do some damage to whatever forms of life did exist there," a space scientists warns. "What's more, all our experiments could be made completely worthless. The tests would show the presence of earthly organisms on Mars or the moon and we could never be sure whether they were there in the first place. We might just have brought them with us."

Until recently astronomers used to say flatly that there was no life at all on the moon. Although our satellite probably had an atmosphere early in its history, it has none now — and no water. Temperatures climb to 212° F. in the daytime and drop to a chilling −356° F. at night. Radiation is at a very high level. How could anything at all live under those terrible conditions?

The more we learn about the moon, however, the less certain we become. It is possible that at the time when the

moon had an atmosphere, microorganisms (tiny forms of life) such as fungi, bacteria and viruses might have developed. They could no longer be growing or reproducing, but they might have survived in a dormant state.

Right here on earth, during bitter cold winters or long periods of drought, some organisms remain quiet or sleeping, waiting for the first touch of spring, the first drop of water. On the moon, to be sure, that never comes. But the microorganisms might have been protected from total death by the rocks and the heavy layer of dust that we now believe cover the surface of the moon. The dust and rocks provide protection against the blistering heat and unearthly cold. It is likely that the temperature beneath these layers stays at around $-30°$ F. Craters and crevasses go still deeper inside the surface and might offer shielding against the radiation from the sun. Even if the microorgan-

isms are completely dead, there might be fossils or remains to show us that they once existed.

Spaceships to the moon are equipped with drills to dig at least a foot and a half beneath the surface. Instruments will analyze everything that comes up. On later trips, scientists will search even deeper within the moon.

Astronomers admit that they are not really hopeful of finding signs of life on the moon. They are not optimistic about Venus either. The temperature on the surface of this planet has been measured at an unbelievable 600° F. This is much too hot to support any kind of life. Even in this case, though, astronomers are not prepared to come out with a firm "no" answer to the question of whether life exists there.

"Venus is covered with heavy clouds," they point out. "The instruments show that these contain carbon dioxide, and all life that we know starts with the carbon atom. The temperature on top of the clouds was measured and was $-30°$ F. It is possible, though not very likely, that some molds or bacteria are floating at the top of the cool clouds."

Most of our hopes are pinned on Mars. The more we learn about this planet, the more likely it seems that we will find living organisms there. Mars has an atmosphere with clouds in it. Through a strong telescope, the planet looks like a big red ball with white caps at the poles. These caps get bigger at some seasons of the year, and smaller at others. About three-eighths of the surface — around the equator of the planet — is a dark greenish color for several months. At other times it turns brown, gray or a brownish purple. What does this description make you think of? Ice caps at the poles that melt in the summer? Green vegetation around the equator that dies in the winter? That is exactly what astronomers have been thinking. Now they are trying to prove it.

Special instruments show that the atmosphere of Mars is mostly nitrogen. It also contains carbon dioxide, more than we have on earth. Carbon compounds have been identified on the surface of the planet. One astronomer has found that the green areas of Mars are made up of elements very much like those in lichens and mosses.

When you stop to consider, Mars does have a number of things to offer a plant. It even has sunlight, about 45 percent of the amount we have on earth. At high noon the light is probably about as bright as it is here in a shaded glen. That is quite enough to set off photosynthesis, the process by which plants grow. There is also plenty of carbon dioxide, the gas that plants breathe in during the daytime. And what of the nights? In the darkness, photosynthesis stops and plants take in oxygen and give off carbon dioxide as we do. Scientists believe that the plants might produce just enough oxygen during the day to supply their own needs at night. There is some water on Mars, but how much remains the big question. The planet is probably very dry. Astronomers fear that the polar caps may just be thin coatings of frost. But even if there are no lakes or rivers to water the Martian soil, some fungi can absorb water vapor from the air.

"Conditions on Mars seem to be particularly well suited to lichens," botanists declare.

As you read in Chapter Two, these plants are combinations of fungi and algae. The fungus part of the lichen could take in water vapor from the Martian air and give it to the algae. The algae part could produce food for both partners by means of photosynthesis and could supply the

123

oxygen needed for the long, dark nights. The fungi could protect the algae from the brutal cold of the night. The temperature varies from a pleasant 77° F. along the equator at midday to far, far below zero at night.

Other primitive forms of life might manage to exist, too. Our climate right here on earth is far from perfect. Just think of the burning heat and dryness of the Sahara desert. It would seem that nothing could live there. And yet a scientific expedition that searched the desolate sands came back with specimens of 28 different species of fungi, 98 species of bacteria and 84 of algae. In other parts of the globe, the thermometer in winter never even approaches the zero mark. Yeasts, molds and bacteria grow there anyway. Some of the bacteria do not even need any air.

"After studying the organisms that live under miserable conditions here on earth, we have made up a list of 18 microbes and primitive plants to look for on Mars," reports a space scientist.

In an effort to figure out which ones the spacemen might find on Mars, scientists have launched a series of dramatic experiments. They have created in laboratories on *earth* conditions just like those on *Mars*. In these "Martian" laboratories, they have placed yeasts, molds, bacteria and other primitive organisms. Now they are seeing which of these can grow.

In one of the tests, these microorganisms were placed in jars filled with nitrogen, the gas which makes up most of the atmosphere on Mars. The air pressure inside these jars was the same as it would be on top of a 60,000-foot-high mountain. That is just about what it is on most of the red planet. The fungi and bacteria had to try to grow in barren soil made of red sandstone and lava. They were denied

Fungi in a "Martian" laboratory.

water. The moisture in the air and soil was held down to one percent or less. The jars were kept at room temperature for nine-hour periods, and then were put into a freezer where the temperature was a bitter $-77°$ Fahrenheit for the remaining 15 hours. The microorganisms had to spend their weekends in the freezer, too. This procedure was kept up for 10 months. Many of the fungi and bacteria could not endure these harsh conditions and died. But quite a number of them managed to survive and even to grow and reproduce. In other tests, microorganisms hung on to life when the moisture was dropped to only four-tenths of one percent.

If they can do it here, they can do it there. At least, that is what we hope. When spaceships land — first without, and then with men on board — we will know for sure.

Scientists are asking NASA to start training biologists as astronauts. They want to be sure that the spacemen will know what to look for and will understand what they see when they set foot on other worlds.

Soil samples will be analyzed chemically and studied under the microscope. Tests will show whether they contain anything alive. Are there organisms which are performing photosynthesis? Are they producing oxygen or carbon dioxide? Can they take in nourishment? Can they grow? Can they reproduce? Are they able to move? If dead now, were they alive once? Are they like anything we have on earth? Are they relatives of the molds, yeasts, other fungi, bacteria, algae or viruses? We expect to have the answers to these questions soon . . . first about the moon, then Mars, then Venus, then the farther planets.

"There may come a time when we will have finished our studies about life on other planets," says an astronomer hopefully. "We may then put some of our useful fungi, bacteria and algae onto those barren soils on purpose. The fungi and bacteria might make the soil fertile so that higher plants could grow. The algae would produce oxygen to enrich the atmosphere.

"All of this will happen in the far distant future — if it happens at all. We like to think that it will, and that colonies on the moon or Mars will seem at least a little like home."

INDEX

127

ABOUT THE AUTHOR

LUCY KAVALER is a freelance writer and has written a non-fiction adult book, *The Private World of High Society,* and two books for young people, *The Wonders of Algae* and *The Artificial World Around Us.* In addition, magazines and periodicals have published her work, including *McCalls, Parents', Today's Living* and *Business Week.*

Born in Brooklyn, a graduate of Oberlin College, she now lives in New York with her husband and their two children, Roger and Andrea.

589.2
Kavaler, Lucy
The wonders of fungi

DATE DUE

DEMCO